PARISH OF LITTLEBURY MILLENNIUM ALBUM

PARISH OF LITTLEBURY MILLENNIUM ALBUM

LITTLEBURY, LITTLEBURY GREEN, CATMERE END AND PARTS OF AUDLEY END

Lizzie Sanders for
LITTLEBURY PARISH COUNCIL

LIFE IN NORTH WEST ESSEX
IN THE YEAR 2000

THE PARISH OF LITTLEBURY MILLENNIUM SOCIETY

To those who gave time

First published in 2002 by
The Parish of Littlebury Millennium Society
North House Littlebury CB11 4TD

© Compilation Lizzie Sanders and Littlebury Parish Council
© Text and photograhy Lizzie Sanders and those acknowledged throughout this book
and on page 263

This book is a copy of the recording made in the millennium year which is kept
in the Reading Room of Saffron Walden Library

ISBN   0-9543910-0-4

Every effort has been made to ensure accuracy in this book. In the event of any error the
author will be pleased to be notified in order to make adjustments to any further edition.

Design by Sally Powell
Printed and bound by Healeys of Ipswich, England

Introduction

This is a record of some of the people and their homes, activities of groups and clubs, and views of the streets and roadsides of the parish taken during this millennium year. Invitations to be part of the album were leafleted to each household, and many villagers volunteered, but where people were too shy or modest, and were particularly recommended for inclusion, some gentle persuasion was exercised, and bore fruit! The album has been financed from the precept and unexpected and generous donations. The 1991 census recorded 277 households in the parish, although this also included Strethall. Here are 88 which should provide a representative picture. It was not the intention to take a census, or write a parish history, rather to let everyone included present themselves as they are this year, as *they* would wish, although it has to be said that most allowed free reign when being photographed, and none the less quite a lot of history has somehow come to be included! Many people have been prepared to write their own words (sometimes these have been added to; the recorder's input is below a central line on the page); and they have been faithfully copied. Otherwise copy has been produced from informal interviews (in these cases the text is marked 'recorder'), subsequently offered back for checking.

All identifying captions read from left to right.

The album is organised as a virtual walk, starting at the crossroads of Littlebury, Littlebury Green and Catmere End, proceeding up through Littlebury Green, turning back at the boundary, down to the crossroads, turning left, up to and around Catmere End, returning along the single track road, rejoining the main road, over the motorway bridge and so to Littlebury.

After Goodwins Close, along Peggy's walk to the railway crossing and back, and the detours to Audley End, the journey proceeds left down the High Street to continue past Clay's Meadow, up the Strethall Road, around Merton Place returning the same way to Kents Yard, and on to the 'triangle', The walk continues around to Rectory Close, out to the village boundary and returns via John's Farm and John's Square, down the Walden Road, over the bridge, across the recreation field and through North End. Again the village boundary is gained on the main road to Saffron Walden and the return is back via the Walden Road, over the bridge, up Mill Lane, turning right up to Church Walk, Church Path, through the alley and out on to the top of the Walden Road once more, around past the The Queen's Head, finally ending at Holy Trinity Church. Littlebury Parish Council hopes that you have an enjoyable 'walk'!

PARISH OF LITTLEBURY, ESSEX

SCALE: 1:25,000

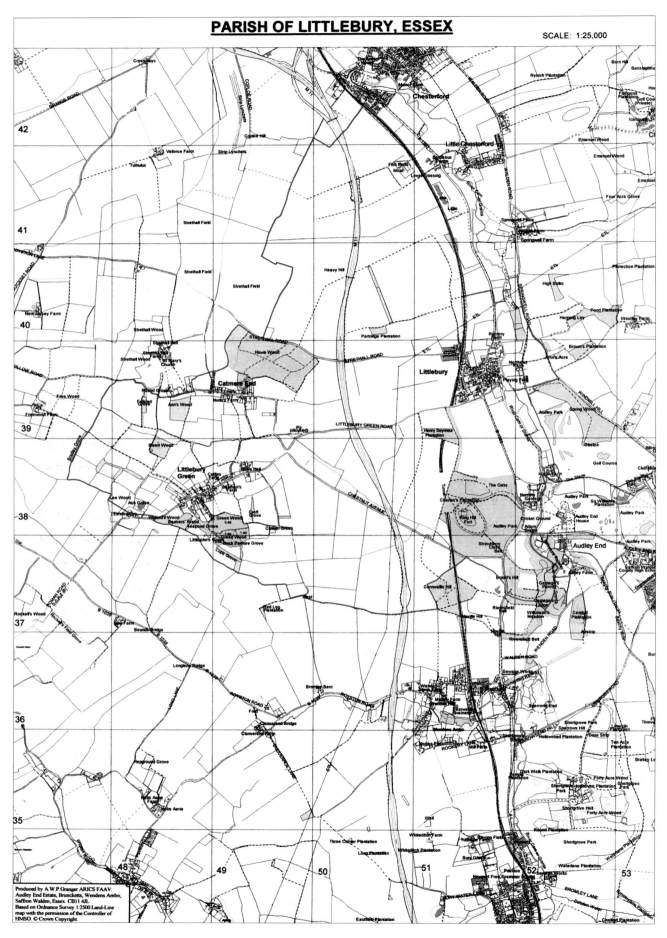

In The Year of 2000

There were New Year's Eve celebrations in 1999 at The Queen's Head, the last and only establishment at the end of 2000 still to be trading (although parts of Clarabel the cow and free range hens' eggs at Kent's Farm @ £1.50 for a dozen are available to a lucky few and wholesalers can continue to buy Army Surplus from PG Wing at Peggy's Walk). But millennium celebrations in the village were mainly private.

In March Laurie Bond, the incumbent vicar moved to Takeley and was not replaced. With him went Dawn, his wife (who had thrilled Littlebury village by opening a twice weekly post office after the shop and sub post office closed), and their children, Cheryl and Simon, first class baby sitters. The year was notable for an unusual amount of rain, resulting in flooding by the river in November. It is sad also to report that vandals damaged some of the stained glass windows in the church, the first time this has ever happened, and syringes were found in the childrens' play area in the recreation ground. The village has sustained these difficulties and can only try to remain vigilant in the face of them.

Littlebury parish has however been assigned a community police officer, Karl Llewellyn, who is keen to be involved, attends Parish Council meetings and makes his presence felt as much as he can, given that he is also a community police officer for five other villages.

The Parish Council, local clubs, societies and committees, fêtes and parish magazine continue to thrive and provide an important link between those that wish to be involved in a village context, and those who are happy simply to be aware that these exist although at present they do not feel the need to participate.

Although from the street there does not appear to be much activity, villagers feel themselves to be part of a community. People are friendly and local events have a graceful social democracy. But as some say, you have to go to the village, not expect the village to come to you, though this does often happen. There is much still to be said for this way of life, changing though it is. The detachment from the town creates community and close bonds, like family it is always there when needed, but like family, care and effort is needed to maintain these.

Littlebury as it was, exists warmly in the hearts of long standing residents, and many of them continue to contribute fully to village life. The village hall would not function as it does or be in such good condition without their efforts.

Holy Trinity Church and St. Peter's at Littlebury Green (which has a dual function as a community centre) continue as a focus for the community because of the efforts of the clergy, the District Church Council, their wardens, caretakers and flower arrangers.

Littlebury parish has beautiful villages and big skies. Open countryside is no more than five minutes walk from any home. Being on the M11 corridor and with Audley End station nearby, communications with London are generally good and the nearby town of Saffron Walden has excellent schools, better than average amenities and fine shopping. It is a very special place to live and bring up a family; many people move here to do just that. The parish of Littlebury has expanded and its social life changed radically in the last forty years following a nationwide pattern. How we fare in the new millennium will be for future generations to judge.

The crossroads

The sheep dip near the crossroads. Audley End Estate have cleaned it out and planted a few trees nearby as a project for the millennium year

Entering Littlebury Green

LITTLEBURY GREEN

Rosie at Little Pen

Harriet, Charlotte Rose (a
friend from Ickleton), Carl,
Jessica, William, and Rosie
at Howe Hall Farm

On Carl's tractor

MR. & MRS. C. JUHL

LITTLE PEN

Carl, born in Ipswich 1958, Rosie, born in Exeter 1956, William, Harriet and Jessica

Carl and I started living in the parish in 1984, his job on the farm has grown over the years from managing six hundred acres to approximately two thousand acres of arable crops. This task he does with two permanent helpers and a number of harvest hands.

We were married at Strethall Church on a cold winter's day in 1992. Yes! I wore my wellies and wedding dress to the 'church in the farmyard', and then we had a reception in the large barn at Nunns Farm and most of the village celebrated with us. It was a wonderful day for us both.

We have now lived in three homes in the parish and have been very happy in each one, out of our three children only Harriet was born at the Rosie Maternity Hospital. Jan Menell delivered Will and Jessie at Nunns Farm and Little Pen respectively. What a joy to have her expert help and wisdom for two special deliveries.

I work at St Mark's College at Audley End organising the catering facilities, it's a spectacular old building, some parts of which are nearly four hundred years old. We have residential accommodation for forty people and on top of this we cater for all sorts of special events.

At present I am a parish councillor which is interesting and enjoyable, the parish has changed over the years we have lived here and I firmly believe that my term as councillor should be for the benefit of my fellow parishioners.

Yes! I wore my wellies and wedding dress to the 'church in the farmyard'.....

MR. AND MRS. T. HAWES

1 HOWE HALL COTTAGES

Terry, Ann, Vicki, Edward and Megan the dog

Coming Home to Littlebury Green

The four of us (five, if you include the dog) have lived in the village for over eleven years.

Coming home from work varies from day to day and week to week depending on where Terry has been working. It ranges from working from our office at home, to commuting to London, to working abroad. If working away, dividing working life and home life begins in Chestnut Avenue, where watching out for traffic gets replaced by watching out for deer, rabbits, pheasants and squirrels. Within the two-mile drive it is possible to make the happy transition from city pressure to countryside/garden leisure.

Edward too, is a daily commuter in his own way, only this time to school in Cambridge. When his friends come to Littlebury Green they know to come in their oldest clothes as they invariably go home covered in mud having gone on many an off-road cycle ride along exceedingly muddy tracks that surround us. Mind you, occasionally, these same teenagers are amazingly transformed and can be seen in their sophisticated 'black tie' outfits ready to take their girlfriends to a local ball.

When Vicki, a student midwife, comes home from Nottingham University/Hospital, the dog knows it is in for an exhausting time with extra long walks the order of the day as Vicki embarks on her relaxation, exercise and fresh air regime, accompanied by her fiancé, Andy. It may be that a bit of home cooking also 'revives the parts that student cooking cannot reach'.

Above all, having good friends and good neighbours puts the icing on the cake!

Terry and Ann

Laura, Alan, Ian, and John

THE MACGREGOR FAMILY

The MacGregor family live at 2 Howe Hall Cottages, Littlebury Green. The family consists of John, Laura, Alan and Iain along with their pets Tosca, a Golden Retriever, Teal, a black Labrador, Jack and Molly their two cats and finally, Storm, a chestnut Quarter Horse.

John was born in Motherwell, Scotland on 19th August 1955. He spent his first twenty two years in his home town of Wishaw. He started working with The Royal Bank of Scotland in Wishaw and worked there for three years followed by a one year stint in Bellshill, another "picturesque" West of Scotland town. He then moved to Edinburgh where he met his wife to be Laura. They married on April 1983. Three years later they moved to New York where they spent six years before moving to San Francisco for another six year spell.

When in California Laura learnt to train horses for any style of Western riding at a friends ranch for future sale. These styles included rodeo and breaking in.

In July 1996 the family moved to Littlebury Green. The reason they moved to Littlebury Green was that they had friends who lived in Ickleton and they therefore decided to concentrate on looking for a house in an area they knew and liked.

Laura Alison Crossan MacGregor was born on 12th September 1963 in Selkirk, Scotland. She spent a number of years in various towns, including Musselburgh, Weymouth and Edinburgh.

Laura is a teacher's assistant at Great Chesterford School. Her speciality is in helping children who need learning support. She did this for two years voluntarily and is now employed professionally.

Alan and Iain were both born in New York. Alan on 19th April 1988 and Iain on 26th June 1990.

ST PETER'S CHURCH

LITTLEBURY GREEN

St Peter's Church fulfills a dual role, that of a House of God and also as a Community Centre. The Churchwardens are Vicky Taylor and her daughter Rose Johnson, they have held this post alternately for many years. In addition to services, this church which is held in affectionate regard by those who know it, houses Parish Council meetings, quiz nights, the children's Christmas party, and can be hired for birthday parties.

The jumble sale overleaf is being held by the St Peter's Community Centre. The Centre helps to pay for the insurance of the church and is currently contributing towards having the heaters serviced. The proceeds from the jumble sale may also go for instance to the elderly at Christmas, bouquets for new babies, gifts for the sick in hospital and welcome gifts to new residents. The committee meet six or eight times a year. The members of the committee who have served and are serving this year are
Chair Jenny Sweet
Secretary Pam Waters
Treasurer Harriet Christodoulides
Penny Coltman
Anne Hawes
Terry Hawes
Rose Johnson
Philippa Scott

special help is given by Sarah Bradfield who stores things in her stables

From Catmere End
Jane Pearson
Michael Pearson

Chris, Rose and James
Johnson and Rose's mother,
Vicky Taylor

Vicky and Rose just before
the Christmas service

Claire Cook, seated at the
right of this picture is
frequently to be seen in
Littlebury Green

Philippa and Jessica Scott

Linda Holt and Penny
Coltman

William and his toy stall

Vicky Taylor, Philippa Scott, Rose Johnson, Penny Coltman, Jenny Sweet, William Holt, Jessica Scott, Linda Holt, Pam Waters and Harriet Christodoulides

Rose, with a welcome cup of tea

Waiting to be allowed in

Penny Coltman at the font, the day before the combined Carol and Christingle service

Vicky Taylor on the same day

Rev Duncan Green, just before the service. St. Peter's felt very special with the beautifully arranged flowers and lit candles. The lights are switched off and the small candles supported by oranges are held by the children standing in a semi-circle while a carol is sung during this service.

THE FLOWER ARRANGERS

ST PETER'S CHURCH

The flower arranging rota stays the same every year. On the day these photographs were taken it was suggested that the only reason the rota would change would be because either someone had died or moved away. The flower arrangers thought that the latter case was the least likely because Littlebury Green is such a wonderful place in which to live !

This year the rota was as follows and is therefore as usual:

January	Rose Johnson
February	Pam Waters
March	Lent, No flowers
April	Ann Hawes
Easter	All help please
May	Lynda Gray
June	Jenny Sweet

St. Peter's Service All help needed! This special service coincides with St. Peter's Day. It is made up of contributions from the congregation, a religious 'show or tell', with hymns and readings. One year the focus was on several silver wedding anniversaries which had coincidentally occurred within the same year.

July	Penny Coltman
August	Can anyone do this month? Pam Waters
September	Jane Bankes-Jones
October	Mary Seymour
Harvest	All help needed please
November	Sarah Bradfield
December	Vicky Taylor
Christmas	All help needed please

For special festivals help is also given by Margaret Osborne and Pat Pratt will also lend a hand and fill in when needed.

Rosie Juhl initiated this photograph to celebrate the Millennium Year. It was taken by Trevor Fry of Debden Green. Tony Sweet set up the photo and is in charge of printing and distribution

Some views of the village,
seen from the road

Local thatcher, Len Osborne's sheep shearing barn

The North West boundary of Littlebury Green

The view from Priest's Cottage on a summer afternoon

Blacksmith's Cottage as seen
from the playground

Howe Hall Cottages

The road as it runs past
Howe Hall

Standing: Philippa, Ruth,
Mike, Jessica, Sarah (sitting)

Mike, Jessica, Ruth Sarah
and Philippa

SCOTT FAMILY

The Scott family moved to 'The Little House' Littlebury from Lewes in Sussex in 1983. Mike's academic position at the University of Sussex had come to an end; a research position at STL in Harlow was the next step. It was mid-winter when we moved in; Ruth was just five weeks old, Sarah three years old, and the main source of heating was a wood-burning stove. It was a difficult start to life in Essex.

Nearly eighteen years on and another daughter later (Jessica, now 16) we are still in the vicinity though now enjoying the rural tranquility of Littlebury Green. 'The Little House' was exactly as the name suggests, and we outgrew it on Jessica's arrival. The main road became busier and noisier and eventually we had to find a larger house: Littlebury Green was an obvious place to look to escape the road, and 'Priest's Cottage' with its large but completely overgrown 'garden', and 'potential for improvement' was what we took on. In those days Mike was a 'Do-It-Yourself' freak and Philippa remains a keen gardener, so it seemed a good choice. It has become a wonderful family home, despite sharing the garden with a wide variety of wildlife, from rats and rabbits to muntjac and fallow deer: regular pruning of roses, clematis and anything tasty is unnecessary here!

As a family we have involved ourselves in many community activities over the years, from toddler and playgroups, Recreation Committee, Friends of Chesterford School, Littlebury Parish Council and most recently St Peters Community Association Committee in Littlebury Green. Our girls have all been educated at local schools and have flourished there. One daughter is now back in Sussex at university, another hoping to go into nursing, and the last studying for GCSEs.

We are a musical family, sporting a cellist, violinist, clarinettist, and a horn player - all of us play the piano, and Jessie is a keen singer. Consequently many of us participate in local music groups: the Uttlesford Orchestra, Walden Sinfonia, Junior Operatic Society, Duxford Music Workshop, school music groups and other ensembles in Cambridgeshire and Hertfordshire.

Despite the fact that Mike's career has moved him to Paignton and Ottawa (Canada) for a large proportion of the year, we hope to be enjoying our house and wildlife garden in the 'mountains of Essex' for many more years to come.

THE SEYMOUR FAMILY

Tim and I did not have any connection with this area before we decided to move here in 1989. I was born on the other side of Essex, in Terling, and then my family moved to Sussex when I was 3. Tim was born and brought up in South Africa, came to Oxford when he was 21, on a Rhodes Scholarship, and has stayed in this country ever since.

We moved here from Wimbledon because we wanted the children to grow up in the country with more space around them. Audley End station was a good place for Tim to commute from to his work in the City. We liked the idea of the proximity of the ancient university town of Cambridge and the charms of Saffron Walden and although the countryside was not as beautiful as some areas of England within commuting distance of London, we felt that it was less crowded and less spoilt by traffic.

We did not have a clear idea about the sort of house we wanted and looked at a variety, in the end coming to live at the Barn. It was converted from a farm building in the 1970s and makes a good home, with a great deal of light pouring through the large windows in the roof. In the garden there is a small barn which we converted into a studio for me to do my etchings in. We can walk straight out of our garden onto an extensive network of public footpaths which we have enjoyed exploring with our dogs, although not necessarily with our children who have almost always preferred to kick a football around the garden than accompany us.

Our children, Matthew, Rosie and Jack, went to school in Cambridge and then away to schools in Kent when they were 13. Matthew is now at Leeds University, Rosie is hoping to go to Edinburgh University in September 2001 and Jack takes his GCSEs in the Summer. When their friends come and stay they often remark on how beautiful the night sky is here. We have no street lights and are four miles from Saffron Walden so we remain free of light pollution.

We have enjoyed the wildlife here and have been very excited over several years to discover kestrels nesting in a hole high up in an old ash tree in the garden. One year an owl took possession and raised two owlets from there. Herds of deer roam in the woods around and, whilst looking most decorative from a distance, they and the little muntjac are extremely destructive when they come into the garden. We have put up quite a high fence to keep them out but the promise of young apple tree bark, tulips in the Spring and tender rose shoots make them determined to find any weakness in the defences.

Mary is a talented artist with
a special skill in etching. her
work is well known locally

Tim and Jack watching
Rugby. South Africa v. Ireland

Sunday morning, Michael
and Harriet

Homework for Joy

LITTLEBURY GREEN. HOME OF THE CHRISTODOULIDES FAMILY

Littlebury Green is "home" not because of its location, or its single main road, or its playground or Church. Littlebury Green is home because of the people who form the village, manage the farmland, provide support to the lonely and comfort to the sad.

We can walk freely along the footpaths, enjoy picking blackberries in the autumn, watch the deer at a distance. We can see the pheasants scuttle from the undergrowth, listen to the foxes bark early in the morning or the owls as they fly on their nocturnal errands. As the sun dips below the horizon and the sky turns a salmon pink we can stand in the twilight beneath the May tree and just see the bats sweep by, on a steady circuit, feasting on the wing.

Littlebury Green has an immense sky. Sky to watch the swallows and martins swoop and climb. Room for the willows, chestnuts and ash to stretch. Sky for the Spitfires, Mustangs, Hurricanes and Hawks of the Red Arrows to recreate old battles or show off new feats. Sky to allow the wind to blow and the leaves to scatter and the clouds to form intriguing shapes of cats, dogs or boats.

We only moved to Littlebury Green in 1990 but our daughter Joy was born in September 1992 so this is definitely "home" to her. To us home is more than the direct family, where one lives or the accumulation of belongings. Home is where one feels a sense of belonging, the opportunity to contribute, the recognition and acceptance that we all have different needs, aspirations, constraints and abilities.

Littlebury Green has an immense sky. Sky to watch the swallows and martins swoop and climb.

GERRY, CLARE, OLIVER AND LAURA MILLICHAP

THE HOOPS

LITTLEBURY GREEN

We originally moved to Littlebury from South London in 1989 to enjoy a more relaxed way of life and also to have a better environment for when we had children. Oliver, who is now 7 years old, likes living here because he enjoys playing football and other games in the garden. Laura is happy playing on the swing and climbing frame. The children both attend school at Dame Johanne Bradbury's in Saffron Walden which used to be the old grammar school. Gerry commutes to London from Audley End railway station and currently works as a trader in the City. Clare works part time in the science department at Saffron Walden County High School.

We moved to The Hoops in 1995 just after Laura was born because we needed more room and loved the character of the house. The Hoops was run as a public house from 1895 to 1969 when it was purchased by a Mr Perkins who converted it into a private dwelling and subsequently added an extension in 1983. The oldest part of the house dates back to approximately 1650.

We all enjoy living here and particularly appreciate the views of the surrounding countryside.

Clare, Laura and Gerry.

Oliver and Laura

Jane is a gifted
needlewoman. Her canvas
work is to be found all over
the house

This Millennium Banner was worked for St. Peter's

JANE, TONY, HENRY & KATY BANKES-JONES

THE OLD ROSE

LITTLEBURY GREEN

We moved here 20 years ago in 1980 from London. Our son Henry was 6 months old. Penny Coltman was the only other mother in the village with a baby.

The house is called The Old Rose because it had been a pub - called The Rose - up until about 1956. It was only a beer house and Vicky Taylor who still lives in the village was the last Landlord of The Rose. Over the years the house has been added to several times but the front door still opens into what was the public bar.

We are staunch supporters of St. Peter's Church as we believe that it is a vital part of the community, especially in its guise as a Community Centre. We are very lucky to have a Church that can fulfil a dual role and all credit must go to Rose Johnson and Vicky Taylor for fighting to keep it open and maintaining it so beautifully. It has been a real pleasure to sew a few pieces for the Church which really should be seen from the inside.

We have two dogs so most people in the village associate me with walking them - there is a thriving dog walking community in Littlebury Green.

Our only other claim to fame is the fact that we live next to Janet Menell who is without doubt the most important person in the village as she is our local Councillor and never stints herself when it comes to serving the Community. She is also an ace midwife and looked after my daughter Katy excellently when she was born!

JANET MENELL

WALNUT TREE COTTAGE,

LITTLEBURY GREEN.

Jan lives with her husband Anthony and a menagerie, her two 'boys' Peter and David have not yet produced the grandchildren that she craves. Peter, a neurophysiologist, is in the land of the software giants, and David is in a Peruvian jungle, a social anthropologist.

Anthony is undergoing treatment for cancer of the prostate but is otherwise in excellent health, cycling five miles a day and this year completes a journey across the Pyrenees that has taken him five years, in short stages. He works from home three days a week and grows vegetables with passion.

The menagerie consists of donkeys, goats, turkeys, geese, peacocks, guinea fowl and a variety of chickens, plus one elderly dog, a Jack Russell terrier. Jan has a problem, nothing she rears is eaten and she cannot resist hatching eggs under her broody bantams. Old hens never die and some are in their early twenties, making an appearance once a day to eat, totter and chat, it would not occur to them to lay an egg!

"We are very blessed to live in these lovely surroundings." The family has moved three times in Littlebury Green, "sunsets viewed from the back of our cottage are breathtaking."

Jan is team leader of the Saffron Walden midwives, working three days a week in the community, a job she loves and will find hard to give up. She started in the area in 1974 as a district nurse and reverted back to midwifery in 1978. She is a nurse member of the Primary Health Care Group.

Local councillor, she has been a member of the Parish Council since 1974 and the local District Councillor since 1975. In 1994 she was Chairman of Uttlesford D.C. and set up the Buffy Bus as a charity, this is a playbus operating throughout the district. She is a member of several organisations, the council for voluntary service, the community safety action team dealing with vulnerable people, and is chairman of the Amenity committee.

Whenever time allows Jan resorts to her own secret passion, writing. One day she hopes to get something published, meanwhile she takes great pleasure in re-writing her own story which she hopes will run and run!!

Jan with her goats

Jan holding Poppet, David holding Bunty, Peter and Anthony

Alan Button who sold Merlin to the family with Cathy

Daisy and May making their own Christmas cards

Humphrey, on the right of the picture

DR. & MRS. H.Q.P CRICK

SUNNYSIDE

Humphrey, Cathy, May and Daisy

Humphrey and Cathy have lived in Sunnyside since1993. They have two daughters, May (aged 8) and Daisy (aged4). Sunnyside was an old bakery for the village.

Humphrey is an ornithologist working for the British Trust for Ornithology. Cathy is a solicitor working part time in Cambridge for Hewitson, Becke and Shaw. The girls attend Dame Johanne Bradbury's School in Saffron Walden. They own Merlin, a little pony, who is used for ride and drive purposes.

Cathy manages to combine work with having a family. She works as a locum solicitor and helps to give a hand in emergencies saying that the hours are good. The school runs a late stay scheme and can cover the children until 6pm which gives her the flexibility she needs. Furthermore Cathy networks with other mothers, this can often mean that the house is full of children, but Cathy loves visitors and to network you must reciprocate!

DR. D. AND DR. A. LORT

CATLIN'S FARM

Littlebury Green has a lot to offer for families. There is a small church, a playground for small children and lots of lovely walks. There are pleasant houses and a happy atmosphere. We do most of our everyday shopping in Saffron Walden but shop in Cambridge when we need clothes. We go to London once or twice a year to shop or go to the theatre.

Our house is an old Tudor farmhouse. We have lived here for twelve years and we extended it 10 yrs ago to make a five bedroomed house. We converted our barn 3 yrs ago into a playroom with extra sleeping accommodation for when friends come to visit. We have a tennis court as all the family enjoy playing at weekends. We have a field and sometimes our neighbour Len puts his sheep in it to graze.

Both my parents are Doctors working in Saffron Walden and Newport. They are very busy and do not have much time off during the week. They often have to work at the weekends and also at night. My sister Emma (13 yrs) and I (12 yrs) go to The Perse School for girls. We travel to school every day by train from Audley End Station. We both enjoy playing hockey and are on the school team. I also play the oboe and enjoy playing in the orchestra. My brother James is at boarding school in Oundle. He is 15 yrs and will be taking his GSCE exams in the summer.

We have an English Springer Spaniel called Hollie. She is a trained gundog and likes lots of walks. We keep a few chickens as we like to eat fresh eggs.

Every year we try and go to the French Alps to ski. My Grannie has a small apartment in St Martin de Belleville which we love staying in. We have all skied since 4yrs old and we now ski faster than Mummy or Daddy. In the summer we holiday in Cornwall or occasionally in Europe by the sea. This year we are hoping to go to Australia and visit the Great Barrier Reef

By Sarah Lort (12 yrs)

James, David, Sarah, Annette
and Emma

Emma, Sarah and James
with Hollie

Thomas, Katie, Robert, Sarah
and James (with Crumble)

Trampolining, James and
Katie

MR. & MRS. R. BRADFIELD

HOWE HALL

Robert, Sarah, Thomas, James and Katie

Bob and I moved to Littlebury Green in 1985. We sold our flat in London and bought our dream house! Fifteen years later we have at last finished decorating! We love our home and its surrounds. Bob and I both come from East Anglia; he grew up and was educated in Cambridge and I grew up in Norfolk, on The Broads. Bob commutes to London daily by train and I work as a physiotherapist at the Saffron Walden hospital.

We have three children, Thomas (13 years), James (11 years), and Katie (8 years). Tom is keen on films, computers, reading and scuba diving. He is at boarding school in Rugby. We think he'll be a film critic when he is older. James is mad about Warhammer 40,000. This is a war game type activity. He puts the plastic combatants together with glue, then he spends hours painting them and then joins with his friends to 'battle'. It is a hobby requiring patience and skill with a keen tactical side when it comes to playing war games! Katie is always on the move. She loves doing things, be it rollerblading, painting, skate boarding or 'chatting'. They are all great fun and we love doing things together.

Family holidays are important to us. In the summer we sail on an old wooden boat on the River Orwell. We take our small dog Crumble with us and he loves the swimming. At other times of the year we try to go to other parts of the country and the world. However, it is always lovely to come home again to Littlebury Green.

...it is always lovely to come home again to Littlebury Green.

LITTLEBURY GREEN WOMEN'S INSTITUTE

The year 2000 was a memorable one for us, not just for the obvious Millennial reasons, but because Littlebury Green W.I. was 21 years old. Among our current 13½ members (the half is a dual member from Huntingdon), we still have some of our founder members.

In keeping with this being a landmark year, we were Convenors for the annual get-together of the Saffron Group of W.I.s, known as the Spring Group Meeting. This was held in April in the Saffron Walden Town Hall, with Rev John Eley, the Cooking Canon, as our speaker and an attendance of almost one hundred. Having booked John Eley, we were concerned to discover that cooking is not allowed in the Town Hall (it sets off the fire alarms!). However, all was well and he gave us an inspired demonstration. It is usual to have a competition and on this occasion it was a set of knitted clothes for premature babies. A total of 79 tiny garments was sent off to the Rosie Maternity Unit.

We hold monthly meetings in St. Peter's Church, Littlebury Green. Our invited speakers cover a wide range of topics from craft to local and natural history. The annual debate in May on Resolutions to be debated nationally at W.I. General Meetings is always lively and well informed; successful Resolutions form the basis of W.I. lobbying to, for example, support rural Post Offices and British farming. Despite our small membership, we are very active, trying to send delegates to meetings of the Essex Federation and the National Federation of W.I.s. We also regularly enter the W.I. Essex County Show with a fair degree of success. In 2000, Littlebury Green members Angela Armstrong and Gill Sonter were respectively 1st and 2nd in the cake baking competition. We have still to win a Co-operative Class, but it is fun trying!

We initiated and still organize a rota of local W.I.s to supply home made cakes to the day centre in Saffron Walden run by the Saint Clare Hospice, a service which, the Hospice tells us, is greatly appreciated by everyone. One of our members, Jenny Sweet, is also very active in the W.I. Market in Saffron Walden.

As often as our finances allow, we give a bursary for one of our members to attend a course of their choice at Denman, the wonderful W.I. College in Oxfordshire. It is an elegant house in beautiful grounds. Members have in recent years studied such topics as signing for the deaf, family history and antique furniture.

We celebrated our 21st birthday with a guided visit, accompanied by husbands and guests, to the Cambridge Botanic Gardens and a meal in Browns. We shall launch ourselves in 2001 with a visit to the pantomime at the Cambridge Arts Theatre. New members are always welcome. The W.I. is not all jam and Jerusalem!

The full membership would also include: Angela Armstrong, Renee Cottingham, Joan Dyer, Jill Hamilton, Rosie Juhl, Isabel Norris, and Pamela Waters. The honorary members are Elspeth Grant and Janet Adams.

Isabel Leeming

This tablecloth has been embroidered with the names of all the members of this W.I.

Gill Sonter; Secretary, Isabel Leeming; President, Jenny Sweet; Treasurer

Jane Pearson,
Gilli Rutherfurd,
Freda Fotheringham
(standing),
Gill Sonter,
Isabel Leeming,
Jenny Sweet,
Margaret Osborne

Across the fields to Howe Hall Farm

Looking north from the crossroads

Towards Catmere End

CATMERE END

PHILLIP, KATE, EMMA, SAM, AND JACK RICHARDSON

LONGACRE,

CATMERE END,

SAFFRON WALDEN,

ESSEX, CB114XG

We first visited Catmere End twenty years ago when we walked the many beautiful footpaths surrounding it. We were living in Saffron Walden then but after a couple of house moves we found and fell in love with Springwood Cottage in the heart of the village. Four happy years and three children later our bees swarmed and Kate rushed after them. She knocked on the door at Longacre and the Cooks kindly let her search the garden and what a garden! It was for sale so, with chickens in dustbins and plants in wheelbarrows we changed homes. And here we have stayed. I first came to North Essex to teach as Head of Art at Friends School Saffron Walden, the job I still have. My children, Emma, Sam and Jack, are now pupils at the school and Kate works at Newport Grammar. House building, card making, picture painting, trumpet practise, homework and looking after our animals and garden take up our time, ... mostly very enjoyably.

She knocked on the door at Longacre and the Cooks kindly let her search the garden and what a garden!

Sam, Emma (standing),
Philip, Jack and Kate

Indoors; Emma, Kate, Jack,
Phillip and Sam, in front

Victoria and Lucy help Liz with Autumn 'tidying' in the garden

Gary, Nick, Lucy, Liz and Victoria

Nick showing his skills on the trampoline

MR. & MRS. G. STOTT

ASH HOUSE

CATMERE END

Gary, Liz, Victoria, Nick and Lucy

We've lived in Catmere End for eight years now and have never had cause to be lonely. Despite the size of this small hamlet of about thirty homes there are as many children. As a result my children always have company when they want it and it is very easy to make friends amongst all the families here. We are not amongst any strangers as you cannot fail to get to know everyone around with regular dog walking and door to door collections!

You can be as involved as you like, ranging from helping in the tiny Strethall Church to fund raising events and concerts, New Year's Eve parties, sailing groupies, hallowe'en gatherings, carol singing, children's Christmas parties, coffee mornings and lots more.

Catmere End is a very peaceful, picturesque village where we are surrounded by good friends and neighbours willing to lend a hand and offer support when needed or just to be there. The doors are always open. What more could you want out of a place to live and bring up your family apart perhaps from a shop, a pub and a bus route!!

Catmere End is a very peaceful, picturesque village where we are surrounded by good friends and neighbours

BILL AND ISABEL LEEMING

We moved to Catmere End from Reading in January 1991. Before long, Mary Leighton (Geoffrey and Mary were then living at Ash House) appeared on our doorstep with a bunch of flowers and an invitation to a Sunday morning drinks party to meet the neighbours - it was a wonderful welcome and has set the tone for our happy 10 years here.

Bill is a carpenter, who decided on closing his small building and woodworking business when we moved. Isabel was then working in research, but has now also (almost!) retired.

Bill is a keen fly fisherman. He is River Warden for the Audley End Fly Fishing Club and a member of Invicta. He belongs to the Probus Club of Audley End. He still keeps his woodworking skills in trim. When we first moved, he helped with projects at the Children's Hospice in Milton and the RSPB bird reserve at Fowlmere. More recently he has taken up instrument making at the Violin Workshop in Cambridge run by Juliet Barker. A viola, violin and cello are complete and a second violin is well on the way. We celebrated Bill's 60th birthday last year with a concert in Strethall Church, three members of the Cambridge University Orchestra playing his instruments. Among the audience were Bill's 3 brothers and one of his 3 sisters and many friends.

Isabel is a zoologist who took her B.A. and D.Phil. degrees at Somerville College, Oxford and is a Fellow of the Institute of Biology. Her work led to a good deal of travel including the splendid year that she and Bill spent at University of California in Berkeley. She is currently President of Littlebury Green W.I., helps in the Oxfam Bookshop in Saffron Walden and is Treasurer of the Victorian Society Great Eastern Group. She is also secretary to the Strethall Church Fabric Appeal set up in 2000.

Mary... appeared on our doorstep with a bunch of flowers and an invitation to a Sunday morning drinks party...

Bill and Isabel

This card, based on a picture by Tony Sweet is sold in aid of the Strethall Church Fabric Appeal

Irene and Garnet

The view across to
Addenbrookes and
the Gog Magog Hills

MR. & MRS. G. TOFTS

THE THATCH

CATMERE END

Garnet and Irene

Garnet and Irene live in one of the highest parts of the parish. The views from upstairs are wonderful. On a clear day Jan Menell's animals can be seen in the Littlebury Green direction ('and the M11, a lovely view! '). From the front of the house, ten miles away the Magog Hills and Addenbrookes hospital are clearly visible and until fairly recently, though now masked by conifers, even Ely Cathedral, thirty miles away could have been seen, especially by night when it was lit up.

It is very quiet here apart from the school bus and the occasional American tourists who having hired bikes in Cambridge knock on the door of this welcoming house for water bottles to be refilled or to receive directions.

Garnet is well known to those who attended the mother and toddlers' group at St. Peter's, Littlebury Green Church, in the early '90s. He regularly brought two of his grandchildren, having taken on their care as Irene was teaching and his daughter in law worked. He also took them for picnics by the river or, for a treat, fish and chips from Sawston. They have six grandchildren now, but Garnet and Irene have gracefully allowed the rest to be cared for by their own mothers, and enjoy some golf and bowls.

The grandchildren patently have a very special place in the hearts and home of their grandparents, they come up a lot in conversation; how they love to sit and chat around the table, or how on entering the house, they are drawn to the 'playroom' a light and warm extension that was built by Garnet and Irene.

The traditionally decorated bedrooms of this happy house, (where even the spiders are protected) are covered by a thatch that was originally put in place 300 years ago. Although maintained and replaced, parts closest to the roof still remain. These ancient rooms provoke thoughts of how many families must have slept in them over the centuries, waking in the mornings to the same fabulous views of Ely Cathedral and the Magog Hills.

recorder

CHRIS AND KATHY WOODHOUSE,

Tim (13 yrs), Louise (12), Susan (10), Katie (8) and Poppy the puppy

We moved to Catmere End from Chestnut Avenue seven years ago, and then 2 years ago we had our new house built on the site of the old bungalow. We love it here and plan to stay forever!

Chris is a chartered surveyor working mostly in London and commutes very reluctantly. He is hoping to be able to work more from home soon.

TIM: I am 13 years old and go to the County High School in Saffron Walden. I get the school bus every day. I like it in Catmere End but I wish there was more to do.

LOUISE: I am 12 years old and I go to the County High. My hobbies are horse riding and ice-skating. I like it in Catmere End but I wish there were some shops. We live in Cuckoo Hill. I also like cooking and drawing.

SUSAN: I am 10 years old and I go to school at Gt. Chesterford and I will go to the County High next year.

KATIE: I am 8 years old and I go to Gt. Chesterford school. I get the bus to school. I like living in Catmere End because my friend is just round the corner.

We love it here and plan to stay forever!

Tim, Katie, Kathy, Louise,
Chris and Susan

Susan with Poppy, Kathy,
Katie and Louise

Jane, Kate, Anna and Molly
(enjoying a better view) with
Peter

Anna and Molly

MR. & MRS. P. FOKS

SANDICOT

Peter, Jane, Kate, Anna & Molly

We like living in Catmere End because:

Kate, 11, "It's all countryside and there's no litter because there aren't any people."

Anna, 8 nearly 9, "There's a field behind our house, with a ditch at the bottom and loads of thistles. "

Molly, 6, "Because it's really beautiful"

"... it's really beautiful"

JANE & MICHAEL PEARSON

We have lived in Catmere End since 1985 and have witnessed the change from a quiet hamlet dominated by the activity of a working farm in a relatively unknown backwater of north-west Essex to a quiet rural hamlet of genteel domesticity with a thirty mile an hour speed limit. Jane is an active member of the Littlebury Green Women's Institute and the Cambridge Soroptimist Club. Michael is a member of the St. Peter's Community Association for the three villages of Littlebury Green, Strethall and Catmere End; is secretary of the PCC for Strethall church and a member of the recently formed fund raising committee to restore the fabric of that church. Michael has worked from his office in the village for the last eight years.

UK PROGRAMME ACTION COMMITTEE
OF SOROPTIMIST INTERNATIONAL

WOMEN WORKING
TOGETHER TO MAKE
A DIFFERENCE

Jane is an active member of the
Cambridge Soroptimist Club

Jane and Michael

In the conservatory

Elspeth

Elspeth and Janet

MS ELSPETH GRANT

HIGH ACRE,

CATMERE END

In 1972 I took over the running of our annual camp for blinded Ex-Service men who are members of St. Dunstan's from a cousin who had run the camp since 1920 less the war years. Since retiring, the camp and St Dunstan's have become a focus in my life. I became a governor of St. Dunstan's in 1995.

The camp caters for from about 45 men though with them all getting older the number has greatly reduced. I have a team of helpers at camp; ex Chief Petty officers, or Petty Officers and their wives and up till two years ago we also had a team of 'dogs' made up from the current Field Gun Crew of the Fleet Air Arm. These were young sailors who gave up a week's leave to come and help. They first came in 1945 and those who come do so year after year and my team of helpers is made up of ex members of the crew.

Until 1995 the camp was held at the Fleet Air Arm station H.M.S. Daedalus at Lee on Solent but when it closed down we were invited to H.M.S. Sultan at Gosport.

I am also a member of the committees for the Dame Bradbury Trust and United Littlebury Charities, a member of the District Church Council and a reader for the Saffron Walden Talking Newspaper.

Elspeth has for four years regularly visited and taken a keen interest in her sister Mrs Janet Adams, M.B.E. who suffered a stroke whilst gardening at their home. Mrs Adams is cared for at Stanley Wilson Lodge and is frail but has an acute sense of humour still. She was a Red Cross Nurse and speaker and was awarded the Florence Nightingale Medal by the International Committee of The Red Cross Society in 1963, their highest award, for '16 years' distinguished relief services in the field'.

Much of her service was seen in emergency situations such as revolutions, the aftermath of earthquakes, and other disasters. She displayed extraordinary bravery, resourcefulness and initiative in her devotion to the sick and wounded. In 1964 Mrs Adams was awarded the M.B.E. for services to Zanzibar and in 1974 was the subject of a 'This is Your Life' television programme.

In her work on the Parish Council her commitment to others continued; Michael Christodoulides said in his article about her in Sign Post Winter 1997/1998 "..she always displayed a concern for the welfare of the community as a whole, whether it be organising the refurbishment of the local pond, planting trees for the future or ensuring clean water is available to travelling families."

Talking about her time in the Yemen in an interview with the Daily Mail in 1972, Mrs Adams said, "In the Yemen I remember zooming along in a Land Rover when one of the Emir's chaps came galloping up. Fired off his musket almost through my hair. It turned out that the closer they fired, the greater the mark of respect".

Metaphorically speaking, fire close.

MR. AND MRS. G. SWAN

George and Betty

George was one of nine children. His family moved to the Old Rectory in Strethall in about 1936 and then to Catmere End in 1950. He spent five years with the Eighth army during the war, meeting up by chance with his brother in Italy. The brothers then ran Swan's Haulage. Sid died this year, he was 73. George retired 13 years ago and his nephew Nigel runs the business now from Strethall.

George is a keen gardener. He does grass cutting and did it at Strethall Church for eight to nine years. His family are buried there. On this wet day the last of a fine show of dahlias give autumn colour through the window. George says that it floods here now where it never used to. Ditches have been filled in to amalgamate fields and hedges removed. In the past roadmen did nothing but clear ditches, trim hedges and roadsides. Now a lot of Littlebury Green water ends up in the River Cam.

George recollects that in the fifties there were only four cottages at Catmere End. Both his sisters in law, Lottie and June still live here in Catmere End, but at this time George is missing Betty who is in hospital.

recorder

...in the fifties there were only four cottages at Catmere End.

George

Whatever the season the
garden is always immaculate

Phyll and Ken

MR. AND MRS. KENNETH MCGRATH

GREENMEAD

'Ken and Phyll'

Kenneth and Phyllis have lived in Catmere End for 24 years. They looked, and found it to be the nearest, nice area to where Ken worked. They have brought up two children who have 'loved it here'. When their son Gary left home he said he wanted to find somewhere equally pleasant. Their daughter Charlotte was married in Littlebury Church where she was a member of the choir and moved to Ely.

Phyll paints and belongs to the Saffron Walden Art Society, she has also belonged to a painting group at Newport for the last twelve years. She and Ken share a love of the garden and enjoy bringing flowers into the house. They still ski in the winter.

Ken explains that at the end of the garden is a wood with an ancient history. Catmere End is the 'Catmere' end of Strethall, and at the time of the Black Death people moved away from Strethall with its church where congregation made contagion possible, Catmere End was set up and a religious order from Ely Cathedral established a community here. There is a double moat in the wood behind Greenmead. One moat remains, and the photograph of the back view of the house was taken from its bank, but there are only traces of the second. There are also Stone Age and Roman remains in the village.

During the last war there was a huge ammunition dump through the woods and a single gauge railway track ran to the main line at Littlebury. The Ordnance corps and Officers' quarters were based at Rose Cottage. In 1946 a plaque was placed on the door bearing the legend 'to be demolished in 5 years', this however didn't take place for forty years!

Ken and Phyll say that the number of houses in Catmere End has not increased in their time here although some have been moved or rebuilt. Ken recollects that when they came the little cottage known as 'The Nest' had earth floors and no running water. It was inhabited by an agricultural worker, Ron, who made a history of Catmere End in words and drawings and this is available still, by special permission at the Saffron Walden Public Library.

recorder

...the little cottage known as 'The Nest' had earth floors and no running water.

MR. & MRS. J.Q. RUTHERFURD

'END HOUSE'

John and Gilli

We are neither of us Essex born and bred, but moved to Saffron Walden in 1965 and to Catmere End in 1978 with three daughters, Alison, Catriona and Olivia (two of them born at home in Mill Lane in Saffron Walden) and two Siamese cats! All the girls were educated at St. Mary's Church of England School and then at Saffron Walden County High. Alison is now married.

John was in the 47th London Infantry Brigade. He was a Captain "for 12 years of undetected crime!", afterwards he worked at B.P. in London and when he retired was treasurer of Littlebury Church for seven years and has worked for the Alzheimer Society for fifteen years and is it's President. He is still Church Warden and Treasurer of Strethall Church. Gillian has belonged to Littlebury Green W.I. almost from its beginning in 1978. She enjoys gardening.

We like being in Catmere End - every approach road is lovely especially Chestnut Avenue in the Spring.

These gates are rather special, they have been designed to open both ways!

Gilli, Kate and John

Looking up the road towards
Strethall outside Ash House

Strethall Church, although
not strictly within the parish,
has strong connections with
Catmere End

Looking back down the road
outside Ash House

Leaving Catmere End

Towards Littlebury

A last glimpse of Littlebury
Green on the left and
Catmere End to the right

Mill lane from the crossroads

The police houses from
Strethall Road

Holy Trinity Church

LITTLEBURY

A first view of Littlebury on the approach from Littlebury Green

Just past Goodwins Close

The flint walls of Granta House on the left and Audley End Estate on the right

Harvesting barley

This field is known as
Shackels Bottom

Cyril Perrin is on the combine
harvester and Tony Appleby
the tractor

Tony at Shackels Bottom

Jane and Tony at home

A DAY IN THE LIFE OF JANE APPLEBY

My days are very varied and really do not run to any set pattern. A farmer's wife is expected to be able to do everything (without grumbling of course!). Tony goes out about 6.45am each morning and takes one of our dogs, Lulu with him, he returns about 08.30am for his breakfast, however at harvest time this can be anytime up to about IO.OOam. Meals are a very disjointed affair with the phone ringing it seems at every meal time!

I enjoy a game of tennis and try to play as much as time will allow, I also enjoy walking and take our older spaniel Lottie out as much as possible.

I am a Churchwarden at Holy Trinity Church Littlebury, which takes a proportion of my time weekends and during the week. Without a resident vicar in Littlebury the job of churchwarden is very important (i.e. to keep the church in good order and to keep all the parishioners in touch with the visiting clergy and the various services).

Tony likes me to be at home as much as possible for telephone calls and sorting the farm bookkeeping. I have been on a computer course and I am now trying to put all that I have learnt into practice.

I enjoy cooking, music and tennis and a large Gin and Tonic!

A DAY IN THE LIFE OF TONY APPLEBY

The weather is responsible for my daily life. As everyone knows the farmer is always complaining about the weather and how it is never what he or she wants! I enjoy my work but I am finding farming increasingly difficult with the change of weather patterns and the involvement of the government telling us what to grow and what not to. I miss the animals, we used to have a large number of pigs and cattle and the farm is not the same without them. Depending on the seasons my day can vary greatly. Harvest time is most demanding, very long hours and often not returning home till late. Autumn always seems to be a rush, with all the winter drilling required to be done as quickly as possible after harvest. This autumn must be one of the wettest on record; work is a long way behind, a lot of frayed tempers and grumbling!

Jane and I moved to Abbey Farm, Audley End in 1990 having spent all my life at Kents Farm, we still feel part of Littlebury although now not actually living there, we still farm the land around the village and take part in village life.

I enjoy walking and reading and like my wife a large Gin and Tonic!

ALAN GRANGER BSC ARICS FAAV

RESIDENT LAND AGENT,

AUDLEY END ESTATE

I am employed by Lord Braybrooke as his Land Agent to manage the Audley End Estate. I live in a farmhouse on the Estate although not actually within the Parish of Littlebury.

I moved to Audley End in March 1993 from Surrey, where I had been managing the County Council's Rural Estate. When I took the position at Audley End I replaced a firm of Surveyors and Land Agents turning the clock back about 50 years to when the Estate last had a Resident Land Agent.

The Estate covers some 7,000 acres in a 'C' shape around Saffron Walden, and Littlebury is quite centrally located. All the farmland within the Parish is owned by the Estate and until the 1950's and 60's the majority of the houses in the Parish were also owned by the Estate. At its peak there were some 300 houses within the Estate. This has gradually reduced to around 70. The Estate is mainly agricultural with a number of farm tenants and in hand farms. In addition to the farms and houses are 500 acres of woods, the Miniature Railway, the Airfield and other property lettings. In total there are some 150 separate tenants/occupiers on the Estate.

I am responsible for the Estate Management and also Lord Braybrooke's own businesses such as the Miniature Railway. There are 17 staff employed on the Estate including within the management team a Farm Manager and Finance Manager. In addition we have farm staff, woodmen, a gamekeeper, building staff, a railway man, office and domestic staff.

I was born in Cornwall, educated in Somerset and went to London University to read Agriculture. Having graduated I travelled around the World for some nine months before studying for my Chartered Surveyors exams. I qualified as a Rural Chartered Surveyor in 1992 and shortly afterwards I also qualified as a Fellow of the Central Association of Agricultural Valuers.

I am married to Catherine and have two children, Lucinda and John born in 1997 and 1999 respectively.

Alan is currently serving as a parish councillor.

Alan at 'Brunckett's' the
Estate office

In the grounds of Audley End
near the woodworking shop,
with the Gate house behind

In the woodworking shop,
where new carriages are
being made for the Audley
End Miniature Railway

Jeffrey and Jennifer at home
in Goodwins Close

MR. J. TWEED

3 GOODWINS CLOSE

Jeffrey and Jennifer

Jennifer is 10 years old and has travelled extensively around the world with her father who recently retired.

Together they spend many happy hours attending the various activities at Audley End House which they often jokingly tell friends 'lies in their garden'!

PETER GORDON WING

profile by Anna Cleaves

I met Peter when I started to come to Beth Shalom in 1992 and his welcoming warmth was one of the memorable features of my attendance at services. I got to know him as a 'self made man', because he told me without rancour that he had no qualifications to his name, other than a scripture prize from school and a certificate of outstanding ability as a ground wireless mechanic.

I felt the warmth of care for people when, unbidden, he said kaddish for my mother in his daily prayers. Peter revels in doing things for other people and he has been a charitable individual all his life. Peter is very proud to have sponsored a rabbinical scholar and he has met many famous people through his extensive charity work. He is to be seen in photographs of charitable events with people such as The Duke of Edinburgh, Jimmy Hill, Terry Wogan and Jimmy Tarbuck. Members of Beth Shalom owe him a debt of gratitude for saving our second night Seder service when it was financially down in the doldrums and contributing, without attribution, to many Beth Shalom occasions.

Born in Holloway, London, Peter describes the year of his birth as the year when Hitler came to power. Peter was adopted within the family because his mother died shortly after he was born. His father was a loving uncle to him because he didn't know that the family had decided that an adoption would be in Peter's best interests and that his parents were actually his grandparents. Peter was orphaned by the time he was eight years old. His mother died when he was only a baby of 10 days old and his father Robert an RAF sergeant, was shot down in the first daylight raid of the war over Germany. His dad's family often called him Bob and until he knew the full story of his adoption it did used to strike him as odd. Peter remembers praying for his dad to come back for years afterwards and when he felt afraid he gained strength from the image of his father as a brave and strong presence whose spirit comforted him throughout his life.

When he was only seven years old Peter was evacuated to Aldrith on the edge of the Fens and he now finds it ironic that he lives so near to this earlier destination. School was somewhat piecemeal, in people's houses, until the end of the war, but Peter was clever enough to win a scholarship to Central school just as his grandparents were finding it very hard to cope with a mischievous eleven year old. Peter remembers doing algebra at the age of eleven and making no progress beyond that in secondary school because the decision was made to send him to an approved school. Far from resenting this Peter looks back at a very positive experience which he describes as being as good as a private boarding school. At school he flourished in sports becoming house captain in his first year and eventually he was chosen to be school captain. Peter achieved high honour in sport. He was Victor Ludorm of the school games and his attendance at boxing club was crowned by his being chosen to represent Britain in boxing.

It was the headmaster of this secondary school who recommended that his adoptive parents tell him the conditions surrounding his birth and at the age of fourteen he discovered that he was born a Jew. He had always known his mother's family and played with his Jewish cousins so that Jewishness was not unfamiliar to him.

When he went into the air force he put down his birth religion and found himself cooking for Jewish, Moslem, vegetarian and 'special diet' servicemen. He was very amused by this because although he knew the specifications for all the diets he didn't know how to cook! He worked in London for Jewish people and picked up Yiddish sufficiently to get his first business break. Peter and his business partner went to a government surplus auction in Colchester and realised that a consortium operating in Yiddish, was keeping a ceiling on the bidding prices. Unfortunately for the consortium Peter understood their plans in Yiddish and the next auction he bid slightly above the ceiling, buying up just about all that was on sale. He remember that day clearly and so does everybody else that was there. A legendary event.

By 1979 Peter was driving a Rolls and owned a large house which he developed and improved, but his success is not just based on fluke but on an immense amount of hard work and the ability to think globally. Peter described himself as a logical thinker, but it is his breadth of vision which has made such a difference to his material success. In 1990 Peter's company received the World-wide International Government Wholesaler of the Year Award by then exporting to twenty seven countries. The local Weekly News described it as a rags to riches story. "That's incorrect", says Peter with a twinkle in his eye, "I was never in rags – my granddad was a bookie!"

Peter's renown has earned him some fascinating contracts. The film called 'Saving Private Ryan' featured 900 helmets which Peter supplied. He kitted out the Robbie Williams dancers at the Brit awards this year finally flogging the white combat trousers that he knew would be totally useless in combat!

Peter's company has taken him all over the world and when he was in South Africa he went to the Torah Academy in Johannesburg where the Lubavitch organization encouraged him to read Torah and become an observant Jew. Peter felt a strong sense of belonging. He learnt Hebrew and to this day he lays tefillin daily.

Peter felt that his profile would be incomplete without mentioning that there has been a new inspiration in his life over the last five years which had brought a depth of contentment that he had never had previously. Peter did not wish to share the details or the sense of this situation which had produced an even greater joy than any he has known.

The warehouse and office beyond the flint cottages

Peter and his staff

Peter says "It is hard to be a winner in a society dedicated to the glorification of losers"

Entering Peggy's Walk

The flint cottages

The railway crossing with Merton Place in the background. There is a path to Merton Place from here

The railway looking towards
the cutting

Near the crossing

Going back to the main road

The entrance to St. Mark's College

John, Liz and Sarah in one of the two courtyards

John, Sarah and Liz playing in Holy Trinity Church

THE WAYPER FAMILY

We came to Littlebury at Easter 1983 from Saffron Walden, where we had spent the first few years of our married life, moving into No.28 Peggy's Walk. We joined the Church and the Team Vicar at that time was Revd. Ian Coomber. We moved to St. Mark's College at Audley End in April 1997, but continued to worship at Holy Trinity.

Liz Wayper

When we first moved I was in full-time teaching as Head of Mathematics at Margaret Dane School in Bishop's Stortford. Church had always been important to me and we worshipped at Holy Trinity regularly from the beginning. I had learnt bell-ringing while at Bishop's Stortford and joined the band of local ringers, which included the Seaman brothers, Roy and Ken, and Cyril Perrin, at that time. I was elected to the Church Council and took on the flower rota. Sarah was born in 1986 and I stopped working in 1987. I took over the running of the Sunday School in 1988 from Ruby Law and became Treasurer of Littlebury Ladies and also Great Chesterford and Littlebury Playgroup in 1988. Since then I have also been Treasurer of the local Girl Guides for three years. At one time I was also the village Avon Lady! As a family we have played music at Family Services, run the Village Praise services and put on various Easter and Christmas children's plays in the church. We have also played for some of the village Christmas parties.

Sarah Wayper

I went to the Mums & Toddlers group when it was held in the Village Hall, then I went to the playgroup, which was in Great Chesterford village hall. I went to school in 1991 in Great Chesterford, where I went into Mrs Bowden's reception class. I joined the local Brownie pack when I was old enough and later joined the Guides. I was in the Sunday School from when I was very little, because my mum was running it then. When I was older, I helped out with the younger children at Sunday School. I play my flute and recorder for Family Services and have played the drums at the Village Praise services.

Jon Wayper

When we moved to Littlebury I was teaching Modern Languages at Bassingbourn Village College and subsequently moved to Sawston VC in 1988 as Head of Languages. I stayed there until 1997, when I took up the post of Warden of St. Mark's College at Audley End, soon after it's reopening as a residential youth & conference centre. I was Churchwarden for several years from the late eighties, serving alongside Cecil Woodley, Max MacGregor, Alastair Lloyd and Laurie Ward. Our whole family played music together for Family Services throughout the incumbencies of Richard Carlill, Shamus Williams and Laurie Bond, aided and abetted variously by Kate Williams and Dawn Bond.

We moved to Peggy's Walk in late August 1998. Our son was then almost two years old and my wife was pregnant with our second child. Prior to our move we had lived in Radwinter Road, Saffron Walden just down from Tesco's. Radwinter Road, although full of character, was 'child unfriendly' both inside and out. Part of the appeal of Peggy's Walk was the actual (and potential) space to raise a family. Since we have been at Peggy's Walk we have extended the house by a third, allowing us the kind of room you need to live together without being on top of each other. Peggy's Walk has good sized gardens both front and back and, being a cul-de-sac, there is little traffic and thus the children have licence to roam as freely as they wish without having to dodge container lorries and Ford Discoverys. Therefore, Peggy's Walk has provided us with those things not available to us at Radwinter Road.

Littlebury itself is a calm if obviously conservative village: very little ruffles its carefully maintained façade unless it is the contented hum of the renovator and decorator. Both our children benefit from living in Littlebury. James, 4, enjoys going to the nursery where he has an ever-growing circle of friends. Frances, 22 months, can't wait to start. The playground is obviously a draw although it doesn't benefit from the excessive rain we have been having recently. The churchyard is a fertile area for hide and seek and the miniature railway at Audley End is tremendous.

We live a comfortable if not benign existence: the dawn chorus is sung by real birds; small children kiss their father goodbye in the morning and hug him on his return in the evening; wild abstract designs cover fridge and kitchen cupboard; Brio train sets vie with piles of marking in the sitting room; cats and squirrels foul the back lawn; the same small children frolic in the mud at the bottom of the garden while their parents idly scan the Sunday papers from the comfort of their living room; meal times are ahum with tantrum and recalcitrance; night time is punctuated with nightmares and moaning. And is there honey still for tea?

Nick Patterson December 2000

Brio train sets vie with piles of marking in the sitting room...

James, Jane, Frances and
Nick

James and Frances

Charlotte, Ian, Timothy (in Ian's arms) and Alistair

Timothy and Alistair

CHARLOTTE, IAN, ALISTAIR (5) AND TIMOTHY (3) DUNHAM.

22 PEGGY'S WALK

From: "Charlotte Cole" <cgc@sanger .ac.uk>
T0: <sanders-art@talk21.com>
Date: Sun, Dec 3, 2000, 5:41 pm
Subject: millennium photo

Within 6 months of moving to Littlebury in Dec 1994 to work on the Human Genome Project at the Sanger Centre (Wellcome Trust genome Campus, Hinxton), Ian and I were married and had experienced crash courses in both parenting and gardening, attempting to nurture both our first son, Alistair (Ally) and our large new garden.

I had moved to a village with some apprehension, having been brought up in a town and spent the previous 10 yrs in London, and insisted on one with a shop. Ian spent his much of his childhood in villages, and after a year of commuting down the M11 to Hinxton, his only concern was to be within easy cycling distance of work and to have a decent pub.

Prior to Ally's birth I had worked full time, and returned to work part-time when he was a few months old. When he was 5 months old, I found myself quite unexpectedly on the Littlebury Recreation Committee (LRC), after being persuaded along to the AGM by my then neighbour, Julie Mason, and for which I have now been secretary for some time. Coping with a first baby who screamed most of the day and returning to work meant that I had not met many people in the village. Joining the LRC proved to be my first real taste of village life, and I'll never forget my shock at the noise at the LRC children's Christmas party a few weeks after I joined. The bonus of finally meeting other villagers and making new friends made any difficulties juggling work/Ally etc worthwhile for me. This in addition, of course, to the playground that resulted from our fundraising efforts - initiated under the enthusiastic and hardworking chairmanship of Morag Coates. Needless to say, Ian may have another view after his greenhouse was taken over for the many fund raising plant sales which followed, along with being surrounded by boxes and accounts associated with the Christmas fundraising catalogue. I hope a bonus for him, though, was me being forced to tackle my poor cake making skills in order to help supply various stalls!

My mother moved from Sussex to Saffron Walden when Ally was 5 months old and Timothy was born a year later in September '97. Being a constant source of advice, friendship and support (as well as ironing!), my Mother's move was a turning point for me and assisted by very regular visits from my sister, Catherine, this helps to re-create the local family support network that villagers of previous generations would no doubt have taken for granted.

Whilst our lawns and hedges are now sadly far less than the perfect ones Adrian and Liz Wright maintained, the garden has become an abundant source of organic fruit and vegetables as well as flower beds. Both boys are keen gardeners and love being outdoors - and I am no longer shocked at the noise young children can make. Ally now attends Great Chesterford primary school with his great friend and fellow Littlebury resident, Matias. Without a shop in the village now, the school bus stop proved to be the second big step towards meeting other village parents. So many of us seem to live frantic lives these days, rushing from one place to another in our cars and it still surprises me how so many people in a small village like ours can be complete strangers for so long.

MRS CELIA ELMER

18 PEGGY'S WALK

Celia and her husband moved to Littlebury from Chelmsford in October 1968. During the time that they were buying the house they took some friends to see it, and Littlebury was flooded! There were only 10 houses on Peggy's Walk at the time and hay and straw were stored at the Atco barns opposite, now there are 20 and P.G. Wing's army surplus store replaces the barns. At that time they suffered from frequent power cuts.

She was a member of the Granta Players and Women's British Legion, and now is a member of the Royal British Legion and the Carpet Bowls Club. Celia assisted with the 'Over 60s' Christmas meal, a tradition which folded a few years ago when those serving began to realize that they were older than some of those being served! There was also afternoon tea held annually in Ray Wright's barns for the over 60s, followed by a mystery tour in a coach, with a raffle. Everybody was very generous and brought a prize, generally the raffle went on for a long time. When entertainers were thin on the ground for the over 60s lunch one year, many husbands decided to bridge the gap in tu-tus and to the tune from the 'Nutcracker' Suite distributed Fruit and Nut bars donated by Cadbury's to everyone.

Pat Penney ran sponsored walks, three that Celia knew of, in aid of Leukaemia research and the last for the NSPCC. Famously, there was a walk on the M11 just before it opened; from Birchanger to Great Chesterford. On the second walk Celia was involved in booking people in, and then went home and got ready to go into hospital. The last walk was 11 miles, from the pump on the triangle, up to Elmdon, and back down to the Lloyds' gateway in Littlebury. And then to The Queen's Head...

Celia has helped with the Littlebury 'Lympics, the five a side football, and still smiles at the thought of John Penney's 'Waterloo' raft (fully described by Brian Sugden). When the Rev. West and his wife left the new vicarage after a popular tenure (he was always seen around, and visited within the week if wanted), The Women's British Legion wished to make them a gift and they settled on a painting of the Mill House by Maggie Davis. Celia also recollects the Rev. Carlill, and how his wife Val ran a Keep Fit class in the village hall to the tune of 'Blackbird Bye-Bye'.

Celia attends most things at the village hall; quiz nights and dances. She doesn't wish to sit on committees, but is always willing to help. She enjoys carpet and outdoor bowls, and, playing in the league, travels around a bit. For carpet bowls this month she is playing at the Working Mens' club in Cambridge, and for outdoor bowls, as part of the Essex League at Castle Hedingham. This is Celia's second contribution to a memorial album, having already appeared as a child in 'Dafen Recollections' by Byron Davies.

recorder

Celia

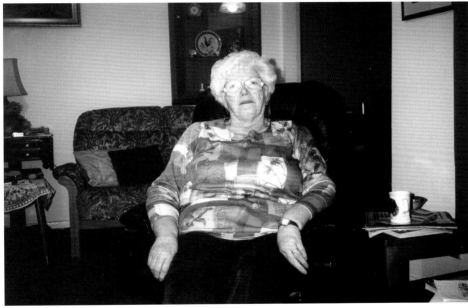

Celia is a keen gardener

June and Bryan

MR. & MRS. B. SUGDEN

14 PEGGY'S WALK

Bryan & June

June and Bryan Sugden moved to Littlebury together with their one year old daughter Caroline in 1964. It did not take long for them to discover if you wanted to be part of village life you had to go to the village and not expect the village to come to you. June became a member of the local Granta players not only as an actress but also prompt, staying with them until it was disbanded. Both June and Bryan served for a number of years on the Village Hall committee and were very much involved with the restoration of the hall in the early seventies. Bryan was also a Parish Councillor for several years. They are both founder members of the Littlebury Carpet Bowls Club. Also Bryan is treasurer of the Littlebury British Legion and chairman of the local Radwinter Bowls Club. June is a fundraiser for this club. During their time in Littlebury two more children, John and Rachel came along, John having the distinction of being the last baby to be delivered by Nurse Clark. Caroline was one of the last children to attend the village school before it moved to Great Chesterford. At this time June together with other parents campaigned unsuccessfully to keep the school open.

Number 14 was the first of the 5 'Rooks' Houses built since the war. When Bryan and June came there was a railway house for the crossing with a siding and Derek Barker's two flint cottages, where he has lived all his life. There was no main drain and no electricity in the streets. Another five houses were built to the left of them in the early seventies and they put themselves on to the main drain at that time. Two sisters, called Mrs Reeves and Miss Taylor ran the post office, in the house now named The Old Post Office; they would open their living room to sell Christmas things and used to deliver to the door if necessary. He also recollects that Mr Reeves' (the chimney sweep) sister gave him his rods when he died. Bryan recalls the Littlebury 'Lympics, particularly one scene in which John Penney (the sports commentator, Walden Road) was seated on the 'loo' reading 'The Sporting Life' and holding up a gin optic - he won first prize. There was five a side football and a Best Dressed Raft competition. Bryan and Adrian Wright, dressed in nightclothes, lay on a raft made from barrels and raced it down the river. During the late sixties and early seventies Cecil Woodley who lived at Forge Cottage organised regular Beetle Drives, also there was Bingo and Whist. One year Bryan and his friends put on an entertainment for the over sixties in which the men, trained by Hilary Stanniforth, did a ballet dance dressed in tu-tus to the music from the Nutcracker suite. When the dance was over the men sashayed through the village hall distributing bars of Fruit and Nut which had been donated by Cadburys. There were regular dances and the village hall committee would have lively discussions about the cost of entry to them. Harry Radley's Band would play and the red composition floor would sweat and bubble up and down with the heat generated from the dancing, making people's shoes and long dresses wet through. The renovation of the village hall started in the late sixties. The work undertaken by willing helpers, both men and women, was organised by the then chairman of the village hall committee, Cyril Lott, who lived in the Gatehouse. The date of this renovation is scratched into the cement just outside the door of the hall. Bryan recollects pulling down the old entrance with a 7lb sledge hammer, it fell into a trench just missing Johnny Kates and knocked down the electric wires plunging half of Littlebury into darkness. Bryan says they had some good times!

Bryan is still working full time as an IT operations manager for Rank Xerox. He enjoys the garden and plays both indoor and outdoor bowls. In the summer Bryan plays in three leagues and June two. Bryan introduced 'Signpost' and edited it for about four to five years and designed the cover, drawing the signpost himself.

MR. & MRS. P. TERRY

10 PEGGY'S WALK

Paul, Katrina (Trina), Ashley, Matthew and Robert

Trina was born and bred in Littlebury, daughter of Cyril and Joyce Perrin and sister to Kevin, Kim and Karen. She is 32, having been born at 2 The Common where she was brought up. It used to be called 2 White Cottages (before it was painted!). Trina worked in the village shop with the Wilbys and then the Ryders, with whom she is still in touch. She met and married Paul having met him when Karen was going out with his brother Peter. David Ryder was Trina's godfather and subsequently Ashley's also.

The Terry family have lived at No 10 for seven years, it is spacious and airy with a large garden and swimming pool. Previously they lived at Bishops Stortford but after three years of travelling frequently back to Littlebury to be with family they returned permanently. Ashley is 8, Matthew 6 and Robert 4.

Trina remembers Church Path and Church Walk when they were fields with 'loads of stinging nettles'. Cyril was well known for his huge prize carrots and displayed them at horticultural shows. Her uncle lived at No 2 with them, only moving out when he married and settled in Linton. Trina does not remember that there were holidays but that they played in the garden for recreation.

Now Trina enjoys her own children; a full time job, they do not allow time at the moment for other activities. Matthew, and Jade (Karen's daughter) are in the same class at Gt Chesterford School. There are only two months between them. The sisters had planned that there should be just three months, but Jade's early arrival and Matthew's late one put paid to otherwise faultless sisterly planning!

recorder

Trina, with Robert and Paul
with Ashley and Matthew

At the 'rec'

Wet weather did not put off John Penney

Penney and Theo Hubbard manning the bottle stall with a delighted Pauline Gale

Alan Green selecting a cake, Ruth Rigby in attendance

Phyll McGrath and Nurse
Clark enjoying an ice cream

The Toy Stall

The Crockery Smash

It's hard to guess whether or not the bottle is full! Paula Spink and Jean Cowell run this stall

Susan Lloyd and Philippa Romer judging the miniature garden competition

The raffle prizes are announced

Cambridge Lodge

The Estate Yard

In Home Farm Yard

The south face of the stables. The Stable Flat is in the nearest part

From the back. In the foreground, Stephen with Ruth, Julie with Danny and Samuel

The view from the flat

MR. & MRS. ELSTUB

THE STABLE FLAT

AUDLEY END HOUSE

Stephen 47 years, Julie 38 years, Samuel 9 years, Danny 7 years, Ruth 3 years

We moved to Audley End 8 years ago from Cambridge. The stable flat has, we believe, one of the best local views across the lawns to the Mansion, Audley End, and Littlebury cricket pitch and the Robert Adam bridge. The Stables are older than the Mansion being built in the mid 1500's. It is the last house in the Parish, the boundary line runs through the grounds.

Steve is Foreman Gardener at the Mansion, Julie is a Community Nurse in Cambridge. Sam and Danny go to R. A. Butler School in Walden and Ruth goes to Saffron Walden Nursery School in Shire Hill.

This weekend we are getting ready for Christmas. After making a late Christmas cake today we will be doing a Tesco's shop before wrapping up some Christmas presents. In the afternoon we have some friends coming over from Cambridge and are going to visit Father Christmas at the Audley End mini-railway on the Estate, an annual tradition for us. We will then have 15 of us for a pre Christmas meal at home. We very often spend time walking in the grounds at the weekends, it's very quiet in winter when the Mansion is closed. We very often see Herons and Kingfishers feeding on the river, as well as the Muntjac deer feeding on the plants!

Sam, Danny and Ruth are all looking forward to the Littlebury Children's Christmas party in the village hall on Sunday.

We wish everybody a very happy 2001

MR. & MRS. A. LLOYD

GRANTA HOUSE

Susan And Alastair

We came to Littlebury in April 1954. There were three working farms and three pubs and the working population was probably 300. We remember hard-working wives who went to the standpipe for water, had no sinks, and did all the washing in a bowl on a table, sometimes outside. The 'Lavender Cart' came round in the morning collecting nightsoil and tin baths were hung outside many cottages. There were seventeen empty cottages; some were condemned because ceilings were too low or because small windows allowed insufficient light and air. Allotments were kept in good order in Church Walk and on the big field to the south of the village.

In 1970 there was a complete change with the arrival of main drainage. Bungalows for pensioners were built at Church Walk and those who were overhoused in Merton Place were moved to them; young families moved to Merton Place and small cottages were amalgamated to make good houses and sold. With two shops Littlebury still remained a friendly place and we believe it is still a very popular village although it boasts no shop and only one pub.

Susan and Alastair have both served on the Church Council for 45 years, 28 of which Susan was 'temporary' secretary. For the last 40 years Susan has been a trustee of the Village Hall, is still Chairperson of the Village Hall Committee and was a Rural District Council member from 1960-74. Taking a keen interest in local education, Susan was the Manager of Littlebury School until it closed in 1971, chaired the governors of Chesterford School for 10 years and was a Governor of Saffron Walden County High School for 36 years where many children from Littlebury have attended.

Alastair served for 40 years on the Parish Council where he has also taken the role of Chair. He has been a member of the British Legion since 1967, and President since 1974. He was Church Warden for 28 years.

Susan and Alastair have brought up four daughters in Granta House, three of whom were born there. The birth of Anne their second daughter was attended by Nurse Clark. They have hosted the Church Fête in their garden for at least thirty years, and have been present at every Littlebury Fête since 1955, but the birth of their first child precluded them from attending the one in 1954!

Granta House has a beautiful garden, which was celebrated by inclusion in 'The Yellow Book' for four years and opened to the public towards the end of June in each of those years. There is much work that has been done for Charity and associated committees that Susan and Alastair will not detail, the benefits of which must be felt by many.

Granta House from the south

Susan and Alastair with 'Beaver'

Susan in the entrance to the courtyard garden

Members of the D.C.C.
Standing, Liz and Jon Wayper, Judy Andrew, Alastair and Susan Loyd, Laurie Ward, Ruth Rigby, Denis Wright and Shirley Green
Seated, Graham Watson, Jane Appleby, Rev. Duncan Green, Rose Johnson and Vicky Taylor
Front row, Mary Seymour, Elspeth Grant, Jane Berney, Mollie Ward and Philippa Romer

Holy Trinity in summer

St. Peter's, Littlebury Green

LITTLEBURY DISTRICT CHURCH COUNCIL

Littlebury is a part of the Parish of Saffron Walden with Wendens Ambo and Littlebury.

Littlebury District Church Council is responsible for looking after the fabric of Holy Trinity Church in Littlebury and St. Peter's Church in Littlebury Green and its members come from Littlebury, Littlebury Green and Catmere End.

In addition and rather more importantly, the D.C.C. (as it is usually known) does all it can to encourage regular worship in the two churches and to look after the needs and welfare of all villagers whether or not they are members of either church.

The Rector of the Parish, Reverend Duncan Green, is the chairman of the D.C.C. and is ably supported by the secretary, Anne Warren, and the Treasurer, Jayne Berney.

Members of the D.C.C. are elected annually in May and anyone who has been confirmed and is on the church electoral roll is eligible for membership.
The D.C.C. meets four times a year either in Littlebury Church or at the various homes of its members. Meets start and conclude with prayers and usually involve a lively exchange of views to better promote the work of Our Lord in the district.

The current members of the D.C.C. (December 2000) are:
Chairman: Rev Duncan Green; Judy Andrew, Jane Appleby (Churchwarden), Jayne Berney (Treasurer), Elspeth Grant, Shirley Green, Rose Johnson (pro-Warden), Alastair Lloyd (Deputy Churchwarden), Susan Lloyd, Ruth Rigby, Philippa Romer, Mary Seymour, Laurie and Mollie Ward, Anne Warren (Secretary), Graham Watson (Church Warden),
John and Liz Wayper and Denis Wright M.B.E.

Graham Watson

THE FLOWER ARRANGERS

HOLY TRINITY CHURCH

As is traditional, the flowers are arranged by a rota. This runs from Easter to Easter and is prepared by Mrs. Wayper. The flowers are changed every week. The volunteers arrange the flowers for the altar vases and the stand in the Sanctuary. If they wish they may also do the stand at the back under the tower, and any others they feel inspired to do. The following tasks are also undertaken: vacuuming the Chancel carpet, sweeping up in the Sanctuary area, and polishing the two brass vases, especially for the first Sunday in the month.

The following parishioners appeared on the rota for this year: Mrs. Andrew, Mrs. Appleby, Mrs. Gale, Mrs. Lloyd, Mrs. Penney, Mrs. Rigby, Mrs. Smith, Mrs. Staniforth, Mrs. Wayper, and Mrs. Ward. Available if required were Mrs. Elmer, Mrs. Finley, Mrs. Lawrence, Mrs. Romer, Mrs. Sugden, Mrs. Warren, and Mrs. Snodgrass. Additionally, arrangers come from Littlebury Green, Catmere End, Saffron Walden and Newport from time to time.

Georgina Day's wedding
day at Holy Trinity

Georgina and Andrew

High House from the
High Street

Theo and Penny with their
daughters, Francesca and
Kinvara, the day after
Hallowe'en

The garden behind the house
is the subject of a lot of work

THE HUBBARDS

THE HIGH HOUSE

When we bought The High House 3½ years ago we did not expect to live here for any period of time. We had escaped from the stresses of living in London and were renting a house in Cambridge. We bought the High House as an investment and let it out. We moved to Littlebury when our tenant left and are here 2 years later! Kinvara our youngest daughter likes the big garden best 'which means she can have a trampoline'. Francesca our eldest likes living in Littlebury because she loves going to the Summer Fête held every year at the Lloyd's House. My husband enjoys the feeling of space and high ceilings which reminds him of the beautiful Adams House he grew up in when his father was a headmaster at a prep boarding school in Bury St Edmunds. I enjoy the wonky walls, the off straight lintels and the character of the House - the fact that it was used as the bomb shelter for the next door school during the war supports my feeling that this House has seen a lot of history. It may not be the prettiest house from the outside but the inside is warm, elegant and interesting.

I enjoy the wonky walls, the off straight lintels and the character of the House...

MR. & MRS. A. BOYCE

MILL COTTAGE

Tony & Jenny, Cary (30), Maryann (27), Anthony (25), Suzanne (17), Liam (15)

Tony and Jenny have lived in the village since October 21st 1981. Two of their children were born locally. Suzanne at Mill Road in Cambridge, before the Rosie maternity hospital was completed and then Liam at The Rosie. Tony comes from Athlone in Ireland and Jenny was born and bred in Saffron Walden. She went to South Road School (where St. Thomas More School now have their playing fields) and then the County High.

The family love the space of the house and garden and the kids love the freedom the space affords. They enjoy car and motorcycle maintenance, Tony has always serviced his own cars but now is finding it harder with his new one because of all the advanced technology that is built in. Anthony has recently stripped down a UNO 608 and rebuilt and resprayed it. He has lowered the springs, given it a full racing kit and converted it into a sports car.

Tony says: Jenny is always busy looking after the family. Since it opened she has worked part time at Tesco's and is very popular with the customers. Starting in '77 Jenny worked as a nursery school teacher for six years, a time she remembers with much pleasure.

Jenny says: Tony has always been in the building trade, and ran his own business. He had government backing for a year, which ceased with the recession. However his skills enabled him to do most of the work on Mill Cottage. Tony can turn his hand to just about anything. This includes taking over the family management if I am working or unwell. He is a good cook! Tony works part time as a D.J. under the name of Mr. B's and also does Karaoke for functions.

Anthony, Suzanne and Liam are the last children still at home. Anthony was born in Jenny and Tony's cottage in Saffron Walden. Liam loves motorbikes and cars, Jenny says he has serviced hers beautifully. He loves music, singing and enjoys football. Suzanne works for a firm of solicitors in Saffron Walden (Stonehams), she has been working for 15 months. She is taking driving lessons and is working hard to take her test. Jenny says she is very creative, making a lot of the family's Christmas decorations and enjoying cookery.

In the past the family have kept many farm animals in their huge garden including Anglo-nubian goats, these would eat anything, even the washing off the line and the hair on your head (hats would sometimes have to be worn)! but they would also give the children rides. One made its way indoors one day, startling the midwife! There have also been ducks, hens (which would hide in the bushes and then re-appear later with a row of chickens) and geese, now just the geese remain.

The family are very happy here, their next project is to restore the barns. Jenny says she loves the countryside, here in Littlebury you are never far from anywhere you want to go. Most days Tony checks on an elderly friend in Castle Camps (who has known Jenny since she was sixteen), and Jenny sends meals for her with him. When necessary Tony drives their friend to keep hospital apointments.

This year saw the celebration of Tony and Jenny Pearl's (thirtieth) wedding annivesary. The family celebrated again, for the millenium this time, at a disco in Newport, run of course by Mr. B's!
recorder

Standing: Liam and Anthony
Seated: Suzanne, Tony and
Jenny

Anthony's pride and joy

The view of Mill Cottage from
the High Street

Sue is a keen gardener

If it weren't for the crazy drivers on the B 1383 it would be perfection.

MR. & MRS. P. WINTERBOTTOM

SQUIRRELS,

HIGH STREET

Phil & Sue

We moved to Littlebury in 1997, having lived in London for over a decade. Phil knew the area already as he had been brought up in South Cambridgeshire. As committed Christians we had asked God to guide us, and everything fell into place for us to buy Squirrels. The beautiful garden created by the previous owner had attracted us to the house. By the way, we've never seen a squirrel since we've moved in! If it weren't for the crazy drivers on the B 1383 it would be perfection.

We are members of Wellspring Church in Saffron Walden, and have made good friends in the area. We appreciate the fresh air, open countryside and accessibility of living here.

Phil and Sue

MR. & MRS. ALDRICH

BEECH COTTAGE

Kenrick, Sarah, Sophie, Jack and Isabelle Aldrich

We moved to Beech Cottage from London in July 1998. The children enjoy having more space and a bigger garden to play in. Sophie the four year old told everyone that we were moving to the country to get away from the smoke!

Kenrick works in the city and Sarah looks after the children and is training to be a Montessori nursery school teacher.

Sophie, six and a half years and Jack, four and a half years were born in London, Isabelle 14 months old was born at the Rosie, Cambridge.

We enjoy life in Littlebury, Sarah is involved with Littlebury Ladies and the recreation ground committee. Sophie and Jack attend Sunday School which they enjoy. Isabelle was christened in Littlebury Church in August.

I moved Here From London When I was four. I Like My verry Big garden. I Like making things. when I grow-up I am going to be a teacher. I Like the playgraund because its fun and exciting. I go to Sunday shool because its fun.

Sarah with Isabelle, Kenrick
and Jack and Sophie seated

Jack and Sophie on their
climbing frame

Littlebury Ladies
Standing: Mary Wright,
Jean Cowell, Lisa Porter,
Ruth Rigby, Judy Andrew,
Sarah Aldrich, Pat Perry,
Shirley Green, Martha
Hughes, Janice Rust,
Joyce Perrin, Ann Warren,
Anne Flynn
Seated: Catherine Berisford,
Olive Law, Nurse Clark,
Betty Shutes, Valerie Green

Rosie Juhl demonstrating the
finer points of cake
decoration

'LITTLEBURY LADIES'

'Littlebury Ladies' meet once a month, inviting a speaker to entertain them. Meetings are open to anyone in Littlebury, and as might be expected, meetings are mainly attended by the fairer sex. Membership is not required.

As Littlebury had no W.I. (although it did have a women's branch of the Royal British Legion which is now incorporated into the men's branch) the group was set up in about 1980 by the Rev. Ian Comber and his wife Jill simply for social reasons, for fun and to provide opportunities to meet other Littleburians. Within a short time of setting up 'Littlebury ladies' the Combers had to leave and the group's fortunes fell into the capable hands of Judy Andrew. Judy particularly recollects the TV personality George Cansdale who dealt with animals and lived in great Chesterford as summoning a good attendance. Also, local historian Mary Whiteman spoke on Littlebury history. This was so popular that Peternella Roberts (then of the Gatehouse) who was hosting the evening had to send out for extra milk for the coffees.

There have always been pancake parties with a beetle drive on the Saturday nearest Shrove Tuesday, and a summer barbecue which grew out of a summer supper, traditionally with strawberries, which used to be held at the vicarage until the Rev. Comber and Jill left, when the event moved to Judy Andrew's house. In twenty years Judy cannot remember rain on this occasion, except for the first time, in this wet Millennium summer. She and Shirley Green ran the group together for about ten years taking turn and turn about as to who was treasurer and who was chair. Currently 'Littlebury Ladies' is jointly chaired by Sarah Aldrich and Catherine Berisford with Pat Perry as treasurer.

The Programme for the Millennium Year

Date	Subject	Venue
13 January 2000	Bruce Munro - Slides of Old Saffron Walden	Valerie's - Stowe House
9 February 2000	Janet Hendy - Tea Plantations in Kenya	Louise's - Cherringtons
8 March 2000	Quiz Night	Jennifer's - Peggy's Walk
12 April 2000	Meal out	The Rose and Crown, Stapleford
10 May 2000	AGM	Anne's - Littlebury Farmhouse
14 June 2000	Blue Badge guided tour of Saffron Walden	Meet at The Common Car Park
12 October 2000	Adam Clemens - Ladies and the Law	Louise's - Cherrington's
8 November 2000	Rosie Juhl - how to decorate a Christmas Cake, You can do more than a snow scene	Valerie's - Stowe House
13 December 2000	Christmas drinks and Quiz	Maddy's - Wheelwright's Cottage

All meetings start at 8pm and cost £1, unless otherwise stated. Please phone Catherine on 528067 or Sarah on 513097 for more details.

THE WILLIAMSON FAMILY

The Williamsons moved to Littlebury in 1990 from Saffron Walden, and before that London. Adrian was originally from North London and Gillian from Nottingham. At the time of the move, they had two children: Mary was three and Patrick one. Thomas was born in 1992. Mary has three pet guinea pigs, Rusty, Abby and Alastair and Patrick has goldfish (from time to time).

In 2000, Mary is at Saffron Walden County High School and Patrick and Thomas in the junior department at St. Thomas More Roman Catholic School in Saffron Walden, where Adrian is also a governor. Mary enjoys dancing, Patrick is a football fanatic and, along with Adrian an ardent supporter of Arsenal, and Thomas loves military history. Gillian is active in the local branch of the Council for the Protection of Rural Essex.

It is amazing how much the Saffron Walden area has changed in the thirteen years they have known it from a relatively sleepy country town to a much larger and more urban-orientated society.

At tea in the kitchen; Patrick, Thomas, Gillian, Adrian and Mary

The back of The Gate House

Gillian's rock cakes are legend

Morag (ironing), Sabrina,
Vanessa, Mark and Tristan

By the Rockola, Mark
and Vanessa, Tristan,
Morag, and Sabrina in front

MR. & MRS. M. COATES

WESTSIDE HOUSE,

CLAYS MEADOW

Mark, Morag, Tristan, Sabrina and Vanessa

Morag Our family moved to Littlebury on Election Day in April 1992 from Theydon Bois. Our reason for moving here was the requirement of more living space to accommodate our three growing children - Tristan, Sabrina and Vanessa.

Little did I realize just how much travel/driving would be involved once living here. To start, my husband commuted to Harrow to work. He left there in December to work in Saudi Arabia for one year whilst I stayed to look after our children and driving to Cambridge and Ashdon to different schools. This pattern of driving lasted until Vanessa joined Sabrina at King's College School. Three children schooling in one city proved a little easier although two journeys a day was the norm. Life appeared to be much simpler when the girls both joined Tristan at St. Faith's. However, over the years the journey to Cambridge has become more arduous with the increase in traffic which goes to Cambridge. As Tristan has now moved on to the Leys School as a home boarder I now make three journeys into Cambridge driving on average approximately 650 miles in a week using 2 tanks of unleaded petrol (130 litres at a cost of 81.9p a litre).

In between travelling I try to do the housework, and gardening which I enjoy but do not seem to have much chance to do properly these days. The children usually ask me to feed their pets during the week. The shopping needs to be fitted in at some point and also looking after the family affairs. However I do try and go to the gym to keep fit and for some sanity! I do play tennis but for the past few months have not been able to fit it in. I enjoy the children's school holidays very much as usually there is less driving involved during peak hours. We like to travel abroad for holidays when we can or visit my parents in Scotland.

My name is Tristan Coates and I am 13 years old Today Tuesday 28th November I woke up 6.30 and ate breakfast. We left to drive to school at 7.25. I arrived at The Leys School at 8.00. We had registration at 8.15 and lessons started at 8.35. My first lesson was French, then a double lesson of design. Afterwards we had a 30 minute break. We then had a single period of geography and then history. We have 40 minutes to have lunch. We then had a single maths lesson. Registration was next and then it is games. This games session we had a match against Kings Ely. We drew 1-1. We had free time after that until 4.50 when we had roll call after which we had free time or an activity. We had supper at 6.00. Free time after that until 6.45 then we go inside our boarding house to do prep until 8.15. Then I went home arriving there at 8.40. I then watched TV till about 10.00.

Hi my name is Sabrina and I am 11 years old Today on 26th November 2000 I woke up and went to watch Gladiator, the film. About half way through I went to have breakfast, then I went back to the film. Soon after that I got dressed and went to my trampolining lesson at 10 o'clock. At 11, when it had finished I went to a shop to buy some food. When I got home I went to clean out my rabbit's hutch then I played on the Nintendo 64. After lunch I went to play on the computer. Soon after I baked a cake with my sister. While it was in the oven I went to watch the rest of Gladiator. When Gladiator had finished I bathed my other rabbit because she was ill. Then I decorated my cake with icing and smarties. Next I went upstairs and wrote a list of people whom I was going to get a Christmas present for and I wrote some of my Christmas list. After that I went to play a bit, also I played on the computer for a while. I then had supper and watched some television. Next I had a shower, said good-night to my mummy and then I went to bed. Goodnight! !

My name is Vanessa. I am nine years old This is what I did on Saturday 25th November 2000. I went to school at St. Faiths in Cambridge. My first lesson was Information Technology. We wrote a poem and did a picture to go with it. Afterwards I had English, we did a quiz and our group got twelve out of fourteen. Then I had playtime and had something to eat. Then I went to the library and I read the Guiness Book of Records 2000. After that we had geography and watched a video about water, my last lesson was Design Technology. I am making a car. I have nearly finished constructing it. I finished school at twelve twenty five. We went to Scotsdales and got some hay and sawdust for my three guinea pigs. I also got some Christmas decorations with a little Christmas tree. I had a Macdonalds for lunch. When I got home I changed and went on the computer for a bit. Afterwards I went to Saffron Walden to buy a birthday present for Olivia as I went to her party at five o'clock - seven o'clock. When I was home I watched some television. Then I did my hair and we went to pick my brother up from school and then I went to Olivia's party. At the party I played football and hockey. For tea we had a hotdog, crisps, crispy cake and tango to drink. At seven mummy came to pick me up and we went home. I got changed into my pyjamas and watched Casualty. After that I went to bed.

DAVID AND PAMELA DAY

"THE SHIELINGS,"

STRETHALL ROAD

David and Pamela were both born in Hampshire where they lived before moving to Essex in the early seventies to enable David to become a partner in a local architectural practice.

Having thoroughly enjoyed their early lives in a small Hampshire village they were attracted to Littlebury and in 1981 moved to Howe Lane, as it was then known.

David's professional qualifications were put to good use almost immediately when he was asked to join the Village Hall Committee in 1982, on which he served for more than 10 years, for most of that time as chairman. He has been a Parish Councillor since 1988 and served as chairman for the two years between 1995 and 1997.

They have two daughters Nicola and Georgina both of whom attended the local schools before progressing to university. They were both married in Holy Trinity Church, Littlebury where they attended Sunday School and Nicola was a helper for a number of years.

David and Pamela's hope for the future of Littlebury in the next millennium is that it should remain a small, unspoilt Essex village.

David and Pamela

The view from The Shielings
over the Strethall road across
the field

Looking up Strethall Road

Annie and Clarabel in the
field in front of Kents Yard

Looking across
to Rectory Close

The approach to the railway bridge

Merton Place

The path from Merton Place to the crossing and Peggy's Walk.

Jean

JEAN COWELL

10 MERTON PLACE

Jean was born at 10 Merton Place and went to Littlebury Endowed Primary School, then to the County High, or Saffron Walden Technical and Modern as it was then called. She was a member of the Church Choir and a Sunday School Teacher. Jean has served on several committees inc: Granta Players (of which she was also a member), Football Club, Over 60's, Silver Jubilee '77, the Cancer Scanner Appeal and Village Hall, the last of which she is still a member.

Jean describes the preparations for the Silver Jubilee celebrations. A committee was formed and a letter sent to all the village committees asking for a small loan (about £10 each was requested) so there were funds to ensure that a day of exciting activities could be presented. An artist Maggie Davis, then living in The Old Post Office painted the outside of her house with a scene of St. George and the Dragon and there was a Best Decorated Cake and Best Decorated Window competition. There was a raffle and the Recreation Committee donated commemorative mugs for children under the age of sixteen. The day began with a service in the church, followed by a lunch in the village hall for the Senior Citizens and meals on wheels for those who couldn't come.

Present at this occasion were the then mayor, Russell Green and TV personality Noel Dyson, who lived in Duddenhoe End. The Mayor was late though and had to have his lunch later! The judging of the windows took place directly after lunch which gave the organisers time to get the celebrations started at the play meadow, (now known as the 'rec'). There was a raffle, Punch & Judy and sports for the children and a Bed Race, all while the windows were being judged. Later on, when everyone had been home to change there was a dance in the village hall with a ploughman's supper. The money raised on the day was sufficient to pay back the various committees who wanted it, and those who didn't allowed those funds to go towards paying for the village sign.

At carnival time in Saffron Walden floats were sent by The Recreation Club, The Football Club and The Granta Players. These were very pretty due to the hard work that went into making the paper flowers and decorations.

Jean's mother helped to start up the village hall, she was a member of The Women's Fellowship which Jean believes was started by the Rev Philip Wright. They had a social evening on Friday nights and whist drives. Jean recollects the Jumble Sales held at the village hall, as a tiny child she was taken by her mother, Dorothy, together with Miss Taylor and Dora Barker to the Mill House to help sort out the jumble in a big room there.

Fêtes were held at August Bank Holiday at this same venue. Cakes were promised to Jean's mother, and Jean was sent out to collect them from neighbours up and down the road. Prior to the teas starting the slabs would be cut into fingers ready to be sold. At Lady Braybrooke's tea was made and washing up performed in the kitchen, but the teas were actually served a considerable distance away, Jean's own tea was often uneaten while she was called upon to ferry china tea things to and fro!

Jean says they were good times, and recalls many passers by stopping in their cars on their way through the village to enjoy a home made tea on an August Bank Holiday. The fête would go on until early evening (about 7pm). In following years there would be Bingo held in the village hall.

Jean is a key member of the Village Hall Committee, she is very keen that the village hall is maintained as a going concern as it is the most accessible focus and meeting point for all villagers. Recalling that the meadow (as well as both Riverside Cottage and Midsummer House) was once so flooded in 1968 that Anne Lloyd and a friend were able to swim in it close to the floodgates she asks, if there were no hall where would people temporarily made homeless by flooding be put in a similar emergency? The church would not be appropriate, but the hall has a variety of uses to which it can be put and without it we would be stuck.

Jean's support of this vital village asset continues. Periodically it takes up a lot of her time, with meetings (though not as many as there were when there was a dance every week and lively discussions took place over the cost of a ticket being increased by too many pence which might result in non-attendance), leafleting and associated commitments. She regrets the change and loss of community spirit, which she puts down to the pressure of modern living. Early starts from, and late returns home mean people haven't the energy on the weekends for village life and are content to do very little. People nowadays have to keep up.

When Jean was fifty, a surprise party was held for her - in the village hall naturally!   *recorder*

Peter and Ann

We moved to Littlebury on July 4th 1978, our independence day from tied cottages. As I like to garden I was not too keen on the soil and garden we moved to. Most of it had not been gardened for several years, it was rough grass, weeds, bed springs, window frames, one ancient lavender, one gooseberry bush.

The soil was so hard I could not get a fork in it. The garden we had before had a rich dark loam, I was not too happy on the new soil I had to work with. When we first moved in we divided the garden into his and hers, his: vegetables, hers: flowers. The vegetables were not so successful due to chalk soil which is very hungry soil for humous, manure from Kents farm soon vanished, the soil was very dry and well drained which a lot of vegetables did not like.

So gradually her took it all over. I now get asked where am I going to find room to put that plant. I am still changing it, the next projects are to put a fence up and grow climbers and wall shrubs that birds and butterflies would benefit from, also a border of different grasses is planned.

Ann's knowledge of growing things is encyclopaedic, and the garden holds a wide selection of unusual plants. Because of the lateness of the season, photographs taken on the day of the visit do not do justice to this plantswoman's collection.

When we first moved in we divided the garden into his and hers, his: vegetables, hers: flowers.

Peter and Ann

Jade and Adam

Adam, Karen and Jade

The gravel garden at No.39

MR. & MRS. P. TERRY

39 MERTON PLACE

Peter, Karen, Adam & Jade

Karen (née Perrin) has lived in Littlebury all her life with the exception of a year in Saffron Walden and 2-3 years in Duxford. She is sister to Kim Bassett (North End) and Trina Terry who is married to her husband's brother.

When Adam was three the Terry family moved to Nettleditch from Duxford (during which time Jade was born) and two years later they settled at No 39., and have lived there happily for four years.

Karen loves Littlebury, all her family and friends are here and she says she could not live anywhere else. Karen has worked in the canteen at Saffron Walden County High School where she was once a pupil. The school is much improved in her opinion since her time there. The children attend Great Chesterford Primary School and say that they love Littlebury for the same reasons as their mother; friends and the family.

Karen regrets the passing of the village shop and post office, as a schoolgirl she worked there when it belonged to Gordon and Sheila Wilby (only minutes away from Mum, Joyce Perrin, who lived behind the church), Trina worked there when David and Geneen Ryder ran it and Karen and Kim worked there with Gordon and Janice Ballard, the last incumbents before it was sold for housing.

recorder

MR. & MRS. P. PARKIN

19 MERTON PLACE

Paul and Georgina

Georgina

Paul and I moved to Littlebury about twelve years ago. I knew this was the right place to live within ten seconds of going into the garden and seeing the spectacular views. Being on the hillside surrounded by open spaces felt so right. One of the benefits of being so high is being able to watch the effects of the wind, something that as sailors we notice all the time.

Sailing is a passion for both of us - we learnt to sail together when we first met and experienced blood, sweat and tears sailing, together with the sheer enjoyment of being outside on the water. We now have our own dinghies as racing together caused too many arguments - each boat has to 'come home' regularly for maintenance or repair, so there is usually one sitting in the front garden waiting for Paul's expertise - the boat is usually mine as I tend to bump into other boats more.

When not sailing or enjoying the views from the garden, there is the 'day job' working for Essex County Council developing services for children and families.

Being on the Parish Council has made me realize how active Littlebury is as a community - there is a great deal going on. Much of the activity is quiet with people 'just getting on with it'. The most important activity the Parish Council is involved with currently is obtaining further affordable housing in the village, so that more families can stay in Littlebury.

Paul

One of my first memories of Littlebury is from our first weekend in the village. I had decided to remove a chimney and spent most of our first week on the roof. The views are stunning - I could understand straight away why people stay here for 40 years or more. One of our neighbours, Bert Nash, had lived here that long, in fact he had worked the land the houses are built on, as a farm worker. We learnt everything we know about gardening from Bert - his front garden was an amazing display of colour every year. Bert's lessons about grouping plants, massing colour and propagation inform our garden now, even though he is no longer around to see it.

My three children have also enjoyed their time here despite the lack of night life!

Littlebury is a special place to live - we hope to be living 'on the hill' for a long time to come.

Georgina and Paul

This year Georgina is chairing
the Parish Council.

Mary and Denis and the view they enjoy from their house

Rev Duncan Green presents Denis with a silver tray to celebrate 60 years as organist at a Trinity Sunday lunch hosted by Graham and Janice Watson

MR. & MRS. D. WRIGHT

27 MERTON PLACE

Denis I moved into the Old Post Office, Littlebury with my parents in 1932. We then went to Hurst Cottage with another Aunt, and Uncle, H.C.Merton, after whom Merton Place was named. My education was at Littlebury School until I left in 1939. In 1934 we moved into the left hand side of Merton Place; we were the first tenants and I joined the Church Choir in the same year. While in the choir I sang 4 treble solos with my uncle, Edward Wright singing the tenor part solo.

After the war broke out in September, Mr Cecil Woodley who was the organist was called up, and that is when I started to play the organ. I was called up in 1943 and served until September 1947 in France, Belgium, Holland and Germany. My last 8 months was in Jamaica.

In 1948 my village activities began. That year I was elected to the Parish Council and Church Council, also sharing the duty of organist, also Sunday School Teacher, which I served for six years.

1949 saw the opening of the Village Hall, where I was appointed a Life Trustee by Lord Braybrooke. As the years passed I went on further committees i.e. The Cricket Club for which I was secretary for 14 years, I was a member of Littlebury Players, also The Over Sixties, which I took over after Mrs Chaplin stood down. I was one of the first trustees of Littlebury United Charities and am now the clerk.

In 1967 the local branch of The Royal British Legion was formed and I was elected Secretary, a post which I still hold. I am Life Vice President of Essex County, was a Group Chairman for 8 years and made a Life Member of The Royal British Legion in 1992.

I served as a Parish Councillor for 51 years during which I was Chairman for 18 years. I was a School Manager (Littlebury) and chairman at the time of closure. With the children going to Great Chesterford School I was elected as one of the governors.

The highlight of my life was when The New Year's Honours List of 1995 was announced. I had been awarded the M.B.E. for my services to the community of Littlebury Parish.

Finally, this millennium year has been a good one. Firstly, Mary and I reached our Golden Wedding, and then on Trinity Sunday, the Church Council presented me with a silver tray to mark 60 years as organist.

Denis recollects the explosion at Ciba Geigy when he worked there in 1974. He was standing at a sink, the walls moved 4 inches and his hand was badly scarred. His injuries were such that he had to take six months off work. It is not known by many that Denis has been called upon to lay people out when they have died and he helps and advises relatives about arranging funerals at a sad and difficult time.

Mary was in the Wrens from May 1943-1946. She and Denis met at the Saffron Walden Co-operative Society during the war where they both worked and they returned to work there after the duration. When she and Denis were married in 1950 they moved over the road to 27 Merton Place which had just been built. Richard was born in 1954 and Sally in 1957, and Mary observes that her aunt lived until she was 104.

Mary helped with the Granta Players and was Secretary and Treasurer on the Village Hall committee when headed up by Lady Braybrooke, who, she recalls, walked up to visit her one day and returned by the steep bank despite the fact that she had broken both her hips in a fall at Waverly Station in Edinburgh and was aided by two sticks. Mary remembers Lady Braybrooke's voice, and it lives on, rendered by Mary as it was with conviction to this delighted and intrigued audience.

BETTY STARR

1, MERTON PLACE,

LITTLEBURY.

Few people have made a greater contribution to the community life of Littlebury than Betty Starr. Her involvement with the Village Hall has been almost a lifelong commitment. She was Secretary of the Village Hall Committee for 23 years and for the last 28 years has been key-holder and care-taker. She has been responsible for keeping the place spick and span for all these years.

She was a founder member of Littlebury Carpet Bowls Club eight years ago and has been its efficient Treasurer all this time. She is an enthusiastic and skilled bowler and has this year taken over the Captaincy of the first team from her grandson. She has also been Treasurer of Littlebury Football Club for the last 15 years and in that time the club's funds have risen to an enviable level of security - not an easy task, for football clubs are famous for being better at spending money than raising it.

But probably Betty's greatest contribution to the community has been her fund-raising, about which fewer people know. She has been Secretary of Saffron Walden Mencap Group and, apart from raising funds for them. has also worked for Milton Hospice, Ida Darwin Ward, Papworth Hospital, Guide Dogs for the Blind and many more. Her estimate of the amount she has raised is £12,000.

In 1998 she received from Uttlesford D.C. their Community Achievement Award, which the village agreed was thoroughly deserved.

Betty has lived in the village for over fifty years and is the head of quite a little dynasty, with three daughters, two sons, six grandchildren and two great-grandchildren.

John Tipton

She has been responsible for keeping the village hall spick and span for all these years.

Bett is a keen bowls player

Maureen, Adèle and Brian

MR. & MRS. B. ASBEY AND MRS. ADELE ASBEY

12 KENTS YARD

Brian and Maureen

Mrs. Adèle Asbey, who is possibly the oldest lady in the village, will be 100 years old next birthday, and lives with her son and daughter-in-law at Kents Yard, Littlebury.

Adèle has 2 children, 6 grandchildren, 9 great grandchildren and 1 great, great grandchild. The Asbeys have lived in various houses in and around Littlebury for the last 30 years. Adèle was born in East London in 1901 and is looking forward to receiving a telegram from the Queen next year.

Mrs. Adèle Asbey has some recommendations for a long and healthy life. Her main motto is 'Everything in moderation' but added to that is to work hard and keep laughing. She remembers horse drawn fire engines and 'did her courting' at Alexander Palace. Mr. Asbey had a butcher's shop and the family moved to Woodford in 1947. They were bombed out twice in London during the war.

Brian moved to Newport in 1971. His family lived in 'The Thatch', now known as 'Thatched Cottage' in the Walden Road, Littlebury from '84 -'86, in Great Bardfield and Duxford from '86 when Adèle joined them - '90, and 'Adèle Lodge' at Catmere End from '90 -'93 (named for Adèle). They had a very sociable time here, Catmere End had and has a very active and social life, in Brian's opinion the best and most friendly in the parish. They moved to Howe Hall Cottages at Littlebury Green in '93 finally settling at Kents Yard in 1997.

This is the only family discovered during the recording for this album who have lived in every village in the parish.

Brian's research in the locality and in particular the houses in which he has lived has thrown up some interesting information. He writes, " On checking my files, Howe Hall (according to Cecil Casbolt, born in Howe Hall Cottages on 15.8.1910), kept before the war hundreds of pigs, sheep, cattle and chickens supplying cream and cheese for the locals, and 60 dozen eggs a week to the market. In those days the fields at Littlebury Green were meadows, and not arable. With regards to happenings in wartime, there was an arms dump on the Chapel Green to Wendens' Ambo track, which always had a couple of soldiers on guard as it held thousands of tons of ammunition. There were also members of the Home Guard stationed by the railway tunnel in Littlebury which was twice attacked by German bombers."

Like many people Brian and Maureen regret the loss of the village shop. They particularly enjoyed going in at Christmas time for the wonderful atmosphere when it was run by the Wilbys. They say that the Wilbys were the best shopkeepers they ever met, they were 'The Village Couple'

recorder

MRS CARMEL CARLINE

CARIAD COTTAGE

Carmel, Blaithin and Killian

We moved to Littlebury in the Spring of 1994. The house we live in was originally a barn. We bought it from the plans and watched it being built with great excitement and anticipation. The original bricks were used in its construction.

We named our home 'Cariad Cottage' which is a Celtic word for a term of endearment. We moved to the village because it was near a small town, schools and airport. We had one child at that time and wanted her to be brought up in a relatively safe and close environment.

Before our second child was born my husband Nick became very ill and died just after Killian's first birthday. It was so apparent during Nick's illness and after his death how many real friends and good neighbours we had. I know there are people at the other end of the phone if I need them, and for that I am truly grateful. Myself and my children, Blaithin and Killian love the closeness and friendliness of the village.

Myself and my children, Blaithin and Killian love the closeness and friendliness of the village.

Blaithin, Carmel and Killian

The view from Cariad
Cottage across the gardens
of Kents Yard

'Cat' with Ellie, Andrew
and Jack with Annie
and Clarabel

Cat in Kent's Farmhouse
Garden

KENT'S FARMHOUSE

LITTLEBURY

SAFFRON WALDEN

ESSEX CB11 4TD

Andrew, Cat, Jack and Ellie Berisford

We moved to Kent's Farmhouse, from Bishop's Stortford, just over five years ago. Littlebury welcomed us with open arms and now Andrew is on the Parish Council and Cat is joint Chair of Littlebury Ladies. Jack (6) and Ellie (4) go to school in Saffron Walden. This year Andrew ran the London Marathon, taking 3½ hours and raising £2,000 for Centrepoint. Many thanks to those of you who very generously sponsored him.

We have two cows, three lambs and seven chickens, which we keep in a rented field, in Strethall Road. We would love to buy a place with land but nowhere we've seen comes with all the attractions of Littlebury - namely excellent neighbours and only a five-minute drive to Saffron Walden.

Post script - we no longer have the cows and sheep in the field - they're in our freezer - and two of the chickens met their "Mrs Tweedy". However we will be re-stocking the field in the spring and, in the meantime if you are interested, the meat is very good and we have lots of it.

We have two cows, three lambs and seven chickens, which we keep in a rented field, in Strethall Road.

PAULINE, STEVE, TIM AND ALASTAIR GALE

We moved to Rectory Close from Newport early in 1984. Tim had just turned two and, to be more accurate, although Alastair was with us, he didn't actually get to see Littlebury until 6 weeks or so later, when he was born !

As is often the case, friendships and contacts were forged with other young families, and soon our involvement with village life started by helping to re-form and run the Recreation Committee and the Mothers' and Toddlers' group. This immersion in village life was further developed through Littlebury Ladies, Parish Council work for a while, and attendance (albeit irregular) of services and Sunday School at Holy Trinity. All of these, but not least the valued friendships and acquaintances we've made, have helped to enrich our 16 years or so in Littlebury.

So to the present, with Pauline still teaching at Chrishall, Steve seeing too much of the M25, Alastair at Saffron Walden County High School where Tim is just finishing the VI form and now playing for Littlebury F.C.

...friendships and contacts were forged with other young families, and soon our involvement with village life started...

Tim, Steve, Pauline and
Alastair in front of the rose,
Francis E. Lester

Steve and Pauline's garden
has many pots and there is
always something flowering

Carol, Andrew, Christopher
and Daniel

Rectory Close from
the Cambridge Road

MR. & MRS. A. C. VINSON

Andrew Vinson moved to 7 North End Cottages in 1960 when his father Brian started work for Mr A D Mclaren of Rectory Farm Littlebury. Andrew attended Littlebury Primary School from 1964 - 1970.

Brian changed jobs in 1970, which meant another change of house to 8 Merton Place. Following in his father's footsteps Andrew spent many hours on the farm and at the age of 14 he was driving a combine harvester all summer long. In 1975 Andrew was offered a farm cottage, 4 Rectory Close in which he remains today.

Andrew met a local Elmdon girl Carole Bates in 1981, and soon found a companion to help care for the orphan lambs and calves. They married in July 1983, and were given a lamb as a wedding present, which they kept in the garden. Unfortunately after only a few months of marriage Carole was Diagnosed with severe Kidney failure and needed to start Dialysis. In July 1986 Carole had a successful Kidney Transplant, and to aid her recovery became Littlebury's local Avon Representative.

In 1989 Andrew purchased his first Tractor and started his own Agricultural Contracting Business based in Littlebury.

Another major event in their lives in 1989 was the birth of their first son Christopher followed closely by the birth of their second son Daniel in 1991.

Andrew finally left working at Rectory farm in 1998 after the death of Mr Mclaren, but at the farm auction they bought a 1929 Gilbert and Barker Petrol Pump as a reminder of their time at the farm. The pump now fully renovated, stands proudly outside their house as a working light.

After nearly 12 years, Carole's transplanted kidney has now failed. Carole is now back on a new type of Dialysis called C.A.P.D. which she does from home 5 times a day herself. Their children, now aged 10 and 8, attend Gt Chesterford Primary School and Andrew still remains a Contractor.

In forty years of living and working in Littlebury, we have seen many changes, but the Community Spirit still remains.

MR. & MRS. D.C. DYER

CAMWELL HOUSE,

RECTORY CLOSE

Derek & Joan

Derek was born at Arkesden. He worked as a Senior Engineer for A.G.B. Audits of Great Britain, a market research company electronically measuring Television Audience Levels. His retirement has enabled him to pursue his absorbing interest in model engineering. He is also Chairman of the local R.A.F Association. During his National Service he worked on Radar and was serving at R.A.F Oakington during the Berlin Airlift.

A qualified teacher, Joan taught in Liverpool where she was born and then Stansted High School, prior to the birth of their two children. Returning to teaching in 1974 she taught at St. Mary's and R.A. Butler schools in Saffron Walden. She became a special needs co-ordinator for N.W. Essex in 1984.

Being also a teacher of the Blind and Partially Sighted (now referred to as Visual Impairment), Joan was appointed as County Advisory Teacher for Visually Impaired students for Hertfordshire County Council in 1987. While in this post she became ill and was diagnosed with Cancer and had to take early retirement in 1994. Her interests now include embroidery, painting and collecting, mainly ceramics. We are celebrating our 40th Wedding Anniversary early in 2001.

Derek and Joan are the very proud parents of Adrian and Catherine. Adrian is a Company Director of Aquasolve Ltd., and Catherine is head of Editorial Research for a publishing company in Cambridge.

We all came to Littlebury in 1982. Now Adrian and Catherine have their own houses not too far away. Our house stood on a completely cleared site and a few days before moving here we stood under the porch with the rain pouring down. Joan noticed a perfect circle of indented soil made by the heavy downpour thereby discovering the site of a well. Hence Camwell House. Cecil and Fred Woodley lived opposite at the Forge and told of the two wells on our site.

We can (from upstairs) see the Audley End Estate over towards the monument and in the summer the village is covered in green foliage. Derek designed and planted the garden. Nowadays we are struggling to keep the foliage at bay, the house in order, and wonder whatever happened to leisure! Of course it is possible we are slower, doing half as much in twice the time!

Joan is a keen embroiderer and has embroidered a kneeler for Strethall Church, secreting inside it a millennium resumé.

Derek and Joan

Mick and Paula

MICHAEL JOHN SPINK - *born South Woodford 11.4.1944*

PAULINE GRACE SPINK *née Midmer - born Wanstead 20.2 1947*
married at Wanstead Baptist Church 14.9.1963

Like all young lovers we dreamt of one day living in a country cottage. Well our dream was realised when we moved to Rose Cottage on the 28th February 1993 from Epping. Like all strangers we were treated with suspicion when we first came to the village especially as Rose Cottage is next door to what used to be the police station. Although at that time I (Mick) was working in London, we spent a lot of time in the Queen's Head just to get to know people and one of the first "locals" to speak to us was young Bill Starr, a better friend no one could wish to have. I stopped working in London in 1995 and it is because of Bill that I am now working at the S.W. Golf Club.

When we came to Littlebury the village hall was very well supported with high attendances at dances etc. Since joining the committee in 1994, we have been involved with clearing ivy, painting the new toilets (that was exciting), improving the kitchen and in our role as entertainment's committee members we have helped with the running of quizzes, variety shows and other forms of fund-raisers. We have also helped with the village and church fêtes, so you can see that we have been kept busy. Unfortunately support for the hall has fallen off in recent times and my one wish for the future is that more people will attend functions especially any newcomers to our village, it's a great way to meet people.

Our latest venture is joining the "Wine Circle" with the idea of tasting and learning about fine wines, silly us, it's just an excuse to get together for an evening of much supping among good company.

On reflection, we think that the past seven years have been the happiest of our lives and that rather than being "in-comers" we feel like, and hope, that we have been accepted as true villagers of Littlebury.

Mick & Paula Spink

MRS RUTH RIGBY

KESWICK LODGE,

ROMAN WAY

My late husband Peter and I moved to Keswick Lodge, Littlebury from Saffron Walden in September '86. We had several friends already living in the village, and since moving we now of course have many more.

When we bought the house, our view from the front door was of cow parsley, buttercups and many trees, with lambs in the field in the Spring. The lambs however, have been replaced with five executive houses!

Peter became a non playing member of the local Cricket Club and we enjoyed a yearly dinner at the Village Hall.

I have been involved in flower arranging at Littlebury Church, and belong to 'Littlebury Ladies', when we meet monthly at each other's houses for a very pleasant evening.

Village life as such has changed quite considerably over the last few years - we now live in a world of technology, but the simplicity of village life will always remain in my memory. As the song says, "They can't take that away from me!"

When we bought the house, our view from the front door was of cow parsley, buttercups and many trees...

Ruth and her roses

Ruth with Brian
Sanders, Mark, a
friend of Judith who
is on the other side
of Gillian Dawson,
Guy Sanders and
Max McGregor,
father of Judith.

Peter and Ruth

Looking in the Cambridge direction

The 'police' house. Dave Ellis was the last policeman to work and live here with his family

Looking south into Littlebury

A view through the farm yard. Maclaren's Farm is owned by Audley End Estate

The Old Rectory, also known as Rectory Farm or Maclaren's Farm has been the subject of much building work and renovation over the year

Back into Littlebury

Judy

Judy Andrew, Sarah
Casbolt, and Kathy
Woodhouse running
Sunday School

MRS. J. ANDREW
CAM HOUSE,
ROMAN WAY

Judy

I came to Littlebury with my husband and four daughters in 1980 rather reluctantly as I was very happy where I was and really didn't want to move. However I was quickly involved in the life of the village. My husband was a Lay Reader and was very soon busy taking services throughout the Deanery. As a family we were involved with the Church in many ways. My third daughter Lisa and then her younger sister Philippa helped in the Sunday School. When Philippa left to go away to college I became involved with the Sunday School and that continues today. For many years I was either secretary or chairlady of Littlebury Ladies but was very pleased finally to hand it over to others.

I am a member of the D.C.C. and over the years have hosted various bible study groups at my house. It has been a great joy to see three of my daughters married in Littlebury Church. But there have been sad times too, as when my husband died in 1996.

Now I am retired I enjoy my garden, the company of my dog, the visits of the various families and grandchildren. This place I didn't want to come to is now woven into the fabric of my life and I can't imagine living anywhere else.

Littlebury Sunday School

There has always been a Sunday School in Littlebury. During the war years it used to meet in the school and then the children would come over to the church to sing in the choir for the services. From 1948 Cecil Woodley and Denis Wright were involved along with others and met on Sunday afternoons in church. During the early '70s it was taken over by Ruby Law and then when she retired in 1988 by Liz Wayper, from that time onwards meeting mainly in the vicarage. But when Laurie Bond our last vicar left just before Easter 2000 the Sunday School had nowhere to go. It meets now at Cam House, Roman Way and the teaching is shared between Jon Wayper, Kathy Woodhouse and Judy Andrew. Our valued pianist is Sarah Casbolt. We have a time of praise and worship followed by a short teaching session geared to the ages of the children and often involving some craft work to take home which is relevant to what they have just learnt. We aim to present the basics of the Christian Faith in an enjoyable, relevant and lively way.

MR. & MRS. P. WALSH

FORGE COTTAGE

Peter, Jenny, Oliver and Rebecca

Peter and I came to Littlebury in May 1990, tempted by the country air and beautiful surroundings. We were keen to get involved in village life, joining various committees including bell ringing!

We started a family in the spring of 1992 and have been blessed with a wonderful son and daughter, Oliver and Rebecca.

As time passed we soon began to realise that our cosy cottage was becoming too cosy, so two years ago we built a family room and have remained happy ever since.

It is hard not to stop and admire Jenny and Peter's 'White' garden

Jenny, Rebecca, Peter and Oliver

The pergola under construction has a Grecian air

Alexander and Kay

MRS KAY MCLAREN AND ALEXANDER

WATERSIDE,

CAMBRIDGE ROAD

Alexander

Alexander has a rabbit called Rhydon - a Pokemon card name. He goes to school at Dame Johanne Bradbury where his father Archie and his brothers also attended. He has had his hair cut for today.

Kay

Kay has a minibus company in London, which she has run for fourteen years. She travels in twice a week. She was a tour guide for nine years and, as American travellers so often asked for a shuttle service, she filled a hole in the market. Kay's company now runs 20 buses. Her clients are tourists, corporate and schools.

Kay met and fell in love with Archie Mclaren junior in Brazil. Kaye was living in London when she became pregnant and they lived together at The Old Rectory for five months whilst expecting Alexander, but were then told that Archie had a brain tumour and had only two months to live. They were married, and against all expectations Archie survived for a further twenty two months, during which time he built a close relationship with his son. Archie died at the age of forty six in August of 1996.

While in remission Archie junior and Kay moved to Rectory Close and stayed there for eighteen months. After he died, Kay bought Waterside within six weeks. Kay says: "It was a confusing time. I felt I should be celebrating the birth of our son, but I was also anticipating the loss of Archie. I felt that I was pulled both ways." Archie's funeral was at Littlebury Church which was bursting at the seams as there were more than three hundred people present, some standing ten deep at the back. He is buried in the churchyard there.

Archie senior, 91, died five months later, waking the night before his own death saying that Archie was calling him. He is buried at Great Chesterford where the family had farmed, and where other relatives are buried. Mrs. Dilys Mclaren returned to her birthplace and is currently living in Wales.

Archie had lived at The Old Rectory all his life and knew everybody. He farmed with his father, Archie senior, and had two other brothers and a half brother. The Mclaren family lived there and farmed the surrounding land for sixty four years. Just before he died, Archie junior stayed in the top right hand bedroom where he had a good view of the comings and goings in the drive. It had always been his dream to buy the The Old Rectory.

A year after Archie's death Kay met Nigel Smith, a farmer and family friend of the Mclarens. She has known him for three years, and together they are building a house in Thriplow.

recorder

PHILIP WATTS,

December 2000

Whilst I spend a lot of my time away from Littlebury there is something always comforting and welcoming about returning to the village at the end of a busy day in the City or a trip abroad. I don't know quite what the charm is. Whether or not it is because I normally only experience the extremes of village life - the busy, rushed and, sometimes, noisy mornings against the more subdued and relaxed evenings. Obviously to return home to one's friends and family always makes the journey a lot more enjoyable!!

Perhaps it's the balanced mixture of village history with that of ongoing development which provides a broad yet stable outlook to life. The richness of an undervalued church which could be so much more a catalyst for village life and, I hope at the start of this new millennium, will be; the special relationship the village has with Audley End Estate and the heritage it provides to so many both local and national visitors; the Queens Head which has seen changing fortunes in past years but which, at last, is beginning to regain the pre-eminent position it once had among local village pubs. Perhaps and most importantly, the fact that a once rural village community has come to terms with an ever changing environment - some of it good and some of it not so good - and a developing cross section of inhabitants, and yet has managed to still retain its own uniqueness and charm.

My warm thanks to the Parish Council for marking such an important turning point in the history of village life. And, many congratulations to the village itself and everybody in it who, in their own particular way, have helped to make this once small hamlet in to a little larger charming and happy village in which to live.

JANE WATTS,

December 2000

We made the exodus up the M11 to Littlebury a little over six years ago and found, thankfully, that village life suited all of us. Although over the past few years there have been the inevitable changes such as the closure of our village shop and latterly our vicar moving to a different parish, there are as always, a small handful of people who strive to keep the village atmosphere alive. This wonderful idea of a Millennium Album is a prime example of this. Thank you.

As a family we always enjoy the social events in the village, which give us the opportunity to get to know our local community. It is always most enjoyable to be so near to Audley End which not only stands in beautiful grounds for walking in but also has a varied and eventful calendar each year providing us with family entertainment on our doorstep. We recently spent a short time living in Saffron Walden but are very glad to be back in Littlebury amongst the many dear and kind friends that we have made over these years. This, for all of us, is what has meant the most about village life in Littlebury.

Hannah, Olivia, Jane and
Philip

These barns are more likely to house a BMW than any animals!

The road past the converted barns: John's Barns

Walden Road

JONATHAN WATTS, *December 2000*

Although I, like my Dad, have spent a lot of time away from Littlebury at boarding school, university and various excursions abroad, it has always been a great relief to come back to Littlebury and the small but active community which has been the backbone of village life.

Throughout my travels I have come to realise that there is nothing that can be compared to a small village community and hope that this friendly atmosphere carries on for many years to come. Throughout the many changes during our time here this community has remained constant and I'm sure we have all benefited from the activities, social events and atmosphere which it has provided.

I'm not sure which aspect of the village I like the most. Probably the smell of open fires during the Winter or the ability of being able to step out of the front door and take the dog for a walk in the fields or at Audley End during the summer. These sights and smells are what I associate most with village life and hope to continue living in such a community for many years to come.

HANNAH WATTS, *December 2000*

My first experience of village life in Littlebury was when I was eleven. It was a big change from living on the outskirts of London, and therefore it took me a while to adjust to the change in scenery. However it didn't take me long to appreciate the lovely countryside and the atmosphere of village life. My first memory of Littlebury was buying huge gobstoppers from the village shop on my way down to the rec to walk the dog, they only cost 3p, sadly something which cannot be repeated by my sister due to the closure of the village shop. Over the years I have had the pleasure of meeting many lovely families through my babysitting that I still enjoy doing today. For me, getting to know so many people in such a short space of time is what village life is all about.

Although I have spent an increasing amount of time in Cambridge due to school commitments and Saturday work, it is always nice to come back to the village where I grew up. I hope this small community remains a unique and friendly village for many years to come.

OLIVIA WATTS, *December 2000*

I like everything about living in Littlebury. I liked the shop when it was there because my Mum used to take me after school and buy either some sweets or an ice cream.

When we lived in Tithe Barn my Dad and I would go on long bike rides through the lanes across the M11 and down the steep hill. Our house was very nice to live in. Some Sundays before the Vicar left we used to go to the church and then we used to go to the pub before having a nice Sunday lunch. Instead of going to church I now go to Sunday School and learn about God, Jesus and his disciples.

On a Monday evening I go to the Ist Littlebury Brownies. I am a Sixer of the Gnomes. We have fun and games and lots of activities. I will be leaving this Christmas because I will then be ten years old.

LITTLEBURY VILLAGE SIGN

This sign was erected FEBRUARY, 1981 to commemorate the Silver Jubilee of Queen Elizabeth II on 7th June, 1977.

From an open meeting held in the Village Hall on Wednesday 22nd September, 1976 plans were made on how to celebrate the Jubilee, a Committee and Sub-Committee was formed as a result.

The Littlebury Jubilee Committee was as follows:-

CHAIRMAN	-	BARRY AUGER
SECRETARY	-	JEAN COWELL
TREASURER	-	KENNETH WORMALD

PAT PENNEY	JUNE SUGDEN	SHIRLEY MARSH	SUSAN LLOYD
SUE KATES	MARGO McGREGOR	MARGARET RIDDELL	BRIAN SCOTT
BILL BADCOCK	CYRIL PERRIN	GEOFF STANIFORTH	IAN PARKER

On Jubilee Day the village saw a lot of activities, a Church service, lunch for the senior citizens, sports and competitions for children and the day finished with a dance.

The Committee had money in hand and some of this was used to purchase trees, (which have since been planted in the Churchyard), then more fund raising events were held, our aim to have something to show future generations, and it was agreed that we had this decorative sign made as our memorial.

The sign was carved by Harry Carter of Swaffam, Norfolk and is one of the last signs to be made by this famous man. He used a drawing of the old Mill as a guide and carved the picture from this. The wood he used was Cedar and the total sum of the sign was £250.00.

With grateful thanks to the following the sign was erected:-

JOHN PENNEY   BRIAN SUGDEN   HILARY ELMER   KEN SEAMAN

plus two Committee members CYRIL PERRIN and BRIAN SCOTT.

Thanks to PAUL PENNEY who transported the sign free of charge and for his valuable assistance with planning negotiations. Also to the residents of Littlebury, who with their help enabled that this sign should become a reality.

. . . .

JEAN COWELL (Secretary)   Friday 13th February, 1981

The mound of flint stones is the old support for the village sign. The new sign is to be replaced within the 'triangle'

A mould of the old sign was taken and remade. The new sign was painted on both sides as it was before by Brian Sanders

Ray Wright made a new post and repainted the letters

Brian and Anne

The view from
the back garden

ANNE AND BRIAN FLYNN

They have lived in Littlebury Farmhouse (formerly Johns' Farmhouse) since 1993 having previously spent seventeen years in Bishops Stortford. The original attraction to the village was the old house and garden. Their family of three is now grown up and has left the nest.

They very much enjoy the village atmosphere and the sense of community which is so strong in Littlebury. Anne is active in Littlebury Ladies and has been chairwoman for the past two years. Brian is a civil engineer and, in addition to the UK, his work has taken them to some of the more remote parts of the globe. He has now been to more than half of the world's countries. They both enjoy travel and Anne has recently been trekking in the Himalayas.

They very much enjoy the village atmosphere and the sense of community which is so strong in Littlebury.

MR. & MRS. M. O'SULLIVAN

THATCHED COTTAGE

Mike, Janet, Robert and Amy

We moved to Littlebury in April 1995. Before then we lived in West London but in the summer of 1994 Janet took a momentous decision and gave up her career as a City solicitor, to take up a Law Fellowship at Selwyn College Cambridge. For two terms we lived apart during the week but this soon became intolerable and we resolved to move out of London.

Mike is a Chancery barrister in Lincoln's Inn and so we needed to move to a village convenient both for Cambridge and commuting to London. We fell in love with Littlebury as soon as we saw the village, and were so thrilled to move to Thatched Cottage, leaving the pollution and unfriendliness of London behind us.

Janet has never for one moment regretted her decision to become an academic lawyer - a career that she loves. She is now a University lecturer in the Cambridge Law Faculty and is Director of Studies in Law at Selwyn. This is the most flexible of jobs, a vital feature since, two and a half years after our move, Robert was born. He is now a wonderful, bright, happy three year old, who is thriving in the Montessori Nursery School in Saffron Walden.

Since this summer photo was taken, we have had a tiny daughter, Amy Ellen, who was born five weeks early in November. Amy is a very special baby - she has Down's syndrome. Inevitably we were initially shocked and saddened to learn of her condition, but very quickly we have also learnt all the wonderful positive aspects of having such a special person in our family. Our neighbours and friends in the village have welcomed Amy in a loving way that has overwhelmed us and we can't think of a better place than Littlebury for Robert and Amy to grow up.

We fell in love with Littlebury as soon as we saw the village, and were so thrilled to move to Thatched Cottage, leaving the pollution and unfriendliness of London behind us.

Mike, Janet and Robert

John and Pat

The garden at St. John's Cottage is always beautiful

MR. & MRS. J. PENNEY
ST. JOHN'S COTTAGE

John & Pat

We moved to Littlebury in February of 1970. Shortly after the worst in living memory, and the last, serious flooding of the river, only to be greeted on the day of our arrival with possibly the worst - and last, serious snowstorm. So; our greeting temperature wise was cold and forbidding. However our greeting from new neighbours around, could not have been warmer.

One good reason for our move here, our eldest daughter Carole had just very recently married, so daughter Tricia, and son Paul came along, and it took very little time for Tricia to marry Terry Wilby, who lived directly opposite, and Paul to marry Sonya Cranston, who lived directly opposite, but in the other direction - two more good reasons for our move.

St John's Cottage which we live in was a broken down thatch, and my lifelong ambition was to live under a straw roof. All too shortly after renovation started we were strongly advised to go for a peg tiled roof, because of the nearness of the road and the impending increase in traffic, and so constant damage to a low overhanging thatch.

This has proved all too right - two good reasons for not coming to Littlebury! However, this set apart, we have had no regrets in moving to this village. A most friendly and happy place to live.

John and Pat's door seems always to be open.

MR. & MRS. A. GREEN

CAMFIELD HOUSE

Alan and Shirley

Construction of Camfield House and Brookfield Cottage

We first came to Littlebury in 1976. After obtaining an amended planning permission for a bungalow and a house in the conservation area, we started building the timber frame bungalow designed by Alan in Spring 1977. As we were opposite the village shop (now sadly gone) we saw people stop in their tracks, last week there was nothing, this week the walls, next week the roof trusses. Visual progress slowed down as it was a 'do-it-yourself' project with help from friends and paid help at weekends. The bungalow was completely finished by August 1978 when Dora Droy, (Shirley's Mum) moved in. She lived there happily until she died in 1985.

Meanwhile we had started building our four bedroomed house, also designed by Alan, with the help of a bricklayer/plasterer who came on Saturdays. Our aim was to build energy conservation properties and the house benefits from some solar heating and extra insulation. It took us two years to make the house habitable. We moved in December 1981 with a heavy snow storm and another two years to complete the interior of the house in time for Christmas 1983.

Over the following years our daughters, Susan and Helen, completed their schooling, went to University, and now live and work away but always enjoy coming back for a weekend and especially Christmas - a very significant time in our family.

One task we are still in progress of completing is the garden. This year's project was the construction of a retaining wall - since nicknamed our flood defences - to separate the lawn adjacent to the house from the area adjacent to the River Cam. Development of this area will continue into next year.

We have always been very pleased that after searching for land for three years throughout Norfolk, Suffolk, Cambs and Essex, the best piece we saw was found in Littlebury and we were able to obtain it and have the satisfaction of building a bungalow and house of our own design.

Alan and Shirley

Building flood defences

Mike and Maureen bought
Folly Cottage in'76 and
brought up Marina and
Damian here

Mike is a media advertising
consultant

Maureen is a textiles expert
and a keen gardener

The Smith family have lived at Midsummer House for 16 years

Emma, Nigel, Pam and (insert) Robert Smith

They love the river and its wildlife; a kestrel lives in the field opposite

Littlebury Village Hall

Littlebury Parish Council

Littlebury Village Hall
Committee

LITTLEBURY PARISH COUNCIL

Each year a precept is set and out of this the Council allocates funds to pay for grass cutting, maintenance of the recreation ground, the war memorial, assistance for the village hall, village caretaker, various insurances, and ad hoc expenses. This year the renewal of the village sign, and the pursuit of affordable housing were on the agenda. The Council also monitors and ensures the maintenance of the verges and lighting in the village. For these things it relies on the co-operation of the District Council of Uttlesford, and benefits in this from the presence of District Councillor Janet Menell. Among other activities this year the Council is trying to have a plan for traffic calming measures made that reflects their wishes.

This year the Council met once a month in Littlebury village hall, excepting April and October when the meeting was held at St. Peter's Church in Littlebury Green.

Shown around the table the Councillors present are: Janet Menell, Tracy Coston; acting clerk, Lizzie Sanders, Georgina Parkin; chairman, Andrew Berisford, Peter Farnsworth, Tony Appleby, Alan Granger. Also serving are David Day and Rosie Juhl

LITTLEBURY VILLAGE HALL COMMITTEE

The Village Hall committee consists of 13 volunteers which also includes the 4 Trustees. Meetings are generally held on a bi-monthly basis. The Entertainments committee however is ongoing to raise funds. This is made up of 4 committee members, Miss J. Cowell, Mr. M. Spink, Mr. B. Starr and Mrs. S. Start plus Mrs. P. Griggs, Mrs. P. Spink and Mrs. C. Harvey. Other sub committees are formed when required to deal with special items like the kitchen refurbishment etc. and they in turn report back to the main committee.

The Trustees are: Mrs. S. Lloyd, Mr. D. Wright M.B.E., Mr. J. Penney, Mr.G. Wilby. The Committee are: Mrs. S. Lloyd; Chairman, Miss J. Cowell; Secretary & Membership Secretary, Mrs. J. Watson; Treasurer

The Committee members are: Mrs. B. Starr, Mrs. J. Clark, Mrs. S. Start, Mr. M. Spink, Mr. M. McGregor, Mr. D. Grinham and Mr. B. Starr

The Entertainment Committee members are: Miss J. Cowell, Mr. M. Spink, Mrs. S. Start, Mr. B. Starr, Mrs. P. Griggs, Mrs. P. Spink and Mrs. C. Harvey

Shown from left to right: Mr. M. McGregor, Mr. M. Spink, Mr. J. Penney, Mrs. J. Watson, Mrs. S. Lloyd, Mrs. J. Cowell, Mrs. B. Starr, Mrs. P. Spink and Mrs. S. Start

THE RECREATION COMMITTEE

The Recreation Committee runs the village children's Christmas party which is held in the village hall. Every child up to the age of ten living in the village receives an invitation, usually this can be coloured in and entered in a competition which is judged at the party. There is a small contribution paid by the parents. The children enjoy games, tea and an entertainer. This is a lively occasion and they always have great fun. In the past carols were also sung led by Jon Wayper, and this tradition is to be revived.

The committee raise funds for the party and also for the maintenance of the play area on the recreation field. In recent years all the equipment has been replaced and safety surfaces laid. Current legislation is very strict and inspections are carried out weekly. The equipment has to be maintained and the committee are hoping to buy some more and also plant a tree to make shade for the summer months. Sadly the equipment has recently been vandalised.

The Recreation Committee contribute to the Parish Council for the maintenance to be carried out, and currently each member also carries personal liability insurance.

Minna Lehvaslaiho: Chair
Charlotte Dunham: Secretary
Andrew Berisford: Treasurer
Sarah Aldrich
Diane Brooker
Nick and Jane Patterson
Lisa Porter
Liz Willstead

Shown at the December meeting are: Andrew Berisford, Liz Willstead, Lisa Porter, Charlotte Dunham, Jane Patterson and Minna Lehvaslaiho

Every child up to the age of ten living in the village receives an invitation

A Recreation Committee meeting

The Christmas party

The Recreation Ground
or 'rec'

John Tipton hosts the Quiz Night in aid of The Village Hall

The Brownies meet once a week. Hannah Watts - Fluffy Owl, Minna Lehvaslaiho - Snowy Owl, Tawney Owl, Claire Green - Brown Owl, Lucy Suckling - Spike Middle Row: Tiffany Clare, Liddie Conway, Charlie Hughes, Erin Quain, Emma Berry, Blaithin Carline, Laura Garland, Vanessa Coates, Hayley McKenna, Olivia Watts
Front Row: Harriet McCaffrey, Thea Quain, Gemma Russell, Ashley Terry, Laura Morgan, Kelly McKenna

Tiny Tots Nursery is run from the Village Hall

The queue starts at least half an hour before this Jumble Sale in aid of the Royal British Legion is due to start

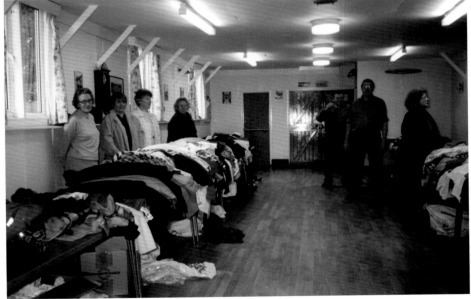

Manning the stalls are: Ruth Rigby, Linda Clark, Jean Cowell, Shirley Marsh, Denis Wright

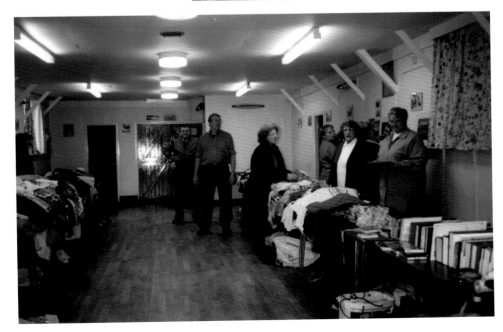

Peter and Ann Dawson, Peggy Griggs, Betty Starr, June Sugden, Jill Kates

The teams pictured are:
Littlebury I Standing: Johnny Kates, Bill Starr, Stan Fanger and John Tipton.
Sitting: Jill Kates, Betty Starr (Captain), Pam Fanger and Shirley Tipton.

Littlebury II Standing: Charlie Allen, Carolyn Harvey, Barbara Mensforth, June Sugden, David Mason and Celia Elmer.
Sitting: Eileen Allen, Laura Snodgrass, Bryan Sugden (Captain), Peggy Griggs, Sheila Thomas and John Snodgrass.

LITTLEBURY CARPET BOWLS CLUB

The club was founded eight years ago with the help of Uttlesford DC Leisure Department who lent us our first mats and woods. But with Betty Starr as our Treasurer and Peggy Griggs as our Secretary we were soon on our feet financially and had purchased our own equipment. As our skills improved we became more competitive and entered a team in the South Cambridgeshire Carpet Bowls League. We now have two teams - one in Division One and one in Division Two of the League. We also play friendly matches against many of the neighbouring villages and each year run a Pairs and Triples Championship. We are a very busy club.

Our Club Night is on Friday, we usually play our home matches on Tuesday and there is another session on Wednesday afternoon, when we entertain some of the more senior members of the village. Our Annual Dinner on the Saturday before Christmas is a noted event in the village's social calendar. Most of our players live in the village, but we have not been slow to recruit friends from the surrounding villages and Saffron Walden to swell our playing strength and add to the convivial atmosphere.

John Tipton

As our skills improved we became more competitive and entered a team in the South Cambridgeshire Carpet Bowls League.

AUDLEY END AND LITTLEBURY CRICKET CLUB

The team in this photograph, on this particular August Saturday, afternoon was:
Back row: Ashley Bower, Blair Meichen, Gary Monk, Adrian Law, Andy Dyer and Fred Phipps.
Seated: Kevin Perrin, James Dyer, Bill Starr (Chairman and Captain for the day), Nick Salmon and Phil Evans.
The Club Captain, Paul Marsh, was unfortunately absent, injured, for this match.

The Cricket Club has entered its third century; research by the club's former President, John Penney, has established that cricket was being played in front of "the big house" as early as the 1880s. There was a traditional link between the game and the residents of the stately homes in the last century. The club can, therefore, be proud to be part of a fine heritage.

Sadly, however, it cannot claim either the size of membership or the level of talent of teams of the recent past. Whereas a few years ago two strong teams were fielded each Saturday in the Cambridgeshire League, now there is only one, as well as a Sunday Friendly XI captained by Peter Lochran. The League results this season have not been very impressive, suggesting that the team may well be relegated to a lower division.

But the news is not all bad. Bill Starr, the energetic and dedicated Chairman, informs us that the club's tenure of the pitch in front of the mansion, which has been in doubt for some time, has at last been settled and that English Heritage has agreed to build them a pavilion on the ground. Bill's comment was, "There will be cricket on that ground as long as I have anything to do with this club."

Although the club draws its membership from Saffron Walden and the surrounding villages, Littlebury is well represented, not only by Bill Starr, but also by Club Captain Paul Marsh and a number of other players, including Kevin Perrin, who is following a fine family tradition.

John Tipton

The Cricket Club has entered its third century

Darrin Marsh

LITTLEBURY FOOTBALL CLUB

The Football Club makes its mark on village life in two ways: if the wind is in the right direction on a Sunday morning the cries of encouragement and frustration from the Recreation Ground can be heard all over the village and at lunch time the Queens Head tends to be crowded with muddy young men.

The club was founded nearly forty years ago to provide sport for the younger men of the village and it grew in size and reputation very quickly. It started by climbing the ladder of divisions in the Cambridgeshire League and then switched to the North West Essex League in which it now competes, with the First Team in the Premier Division and the Reserve Team in Division One.

The club has one of the strongest Sunday teams in the area - it is usually either Champion or Runner-Up in its League, often appears in local Cup Finals and has on two occasions recently represented the district in the finals of the Essex Junior Cup. The Reserves too usually win the League's Reserve Team Trophy. This depth of talent obviously cannot all come from the village, but players are attracted from the surrounding towns and villages by the style and standard of play of the team. Local talent is encouraged, however, and it is pleasing to see two promising village teenagers, Tim Gale and Paul Bassett, making their mark in the Reserves.

But it is still very much a village club. Darrin Marsh is the First Team Manager and his brother, Paul, was for a long time the industrious and popular Secretary, until he gave up the post to devote more time to his family. John Tipton is the Chairman, Betty Starr the Treasurer and Cyril Perrin has only recently been elected Secretary. The ground, which is the envy of much more senior clubs, is looked after most efficiently by Cyril and Adrian Long.

The team featured in the photograph is the First Team at half time during one of its recent matches. It was hoped to include a picture of the Reserves too, but their games in recent weeks have been persistently postponed, due to the appalling quantity of rainfall flooding the pitch.

John Tipton

...on a Sunday morning the cries of encouragement and frustration from the Recreation Ground can be heard all over the village...

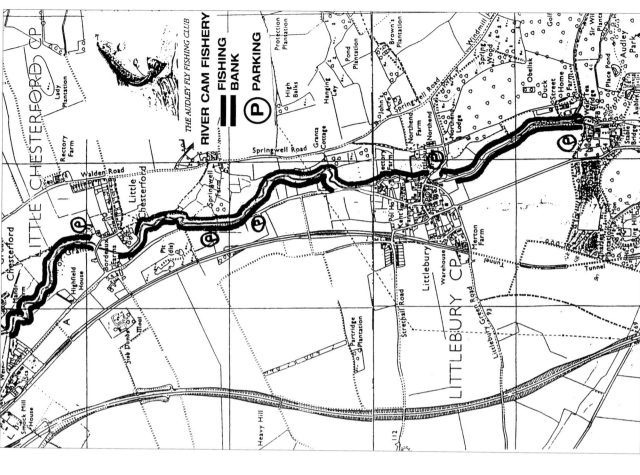

RIVER CAM FISHERY

▬ FISHING
▬ BANK
Ⓟ PARKING

THE AUDLEY FLY FISHING CLUB

HINTS AND SUGGESTIONS FOR THE RIVER CAM

Brown Trout Fishery

Fly Life on The River Cam.

Unlike the richer waters of the southern chalk streams, our rivers have a relatively restricted insect fauna due mainly to the slower flow rates and higher levels of silt. However, most of the common species of aquatic insects are represented.

There is a dominance of Sedge (Caddis) species (at least eight), Caenis and midge / gnat species. Olives (Baetidae) are present but not always in large hatches. Those more commonly seen are the Large dark, Small dark, Pale watery, Blue winged and Medium Olives. Very small hatches of Mayflies have been seen in the last three seasons.

A broad range of terrestrial insects can be found in different months including Hawthorn flies, Black Gnats, Reed Smuts and Midges.

On the River Cam a fairly restricted number of patterns work well and are best fished on smaller hook sizes.

Suggested patterns:-

Nymphs Pheasant Tail, GRHE, Collyers green or brown, Amber nymphs and small buzzers.

Sedges Various patterns

Dry Flies Pheasent Tail dry, GRHE dry, Kite's Imperial, Rough Olive, Pale Watery Dun.
Hawthorn Fly, Black Gnat, Grey Duster, Adams.

HAPPY FISHING AND TIGHT LINES.

Audley Fly Fishing Club

Electro-fishing coarse fish in front of the Mill House on the River Cam

The work of keeping the river clear of weed and debris continues throughout the year

This sign mystifies locals too!

The bridge has been designated unsafe for large vehicles. It is due to be reinforced very soon.

Across the playing field.

Looking across to North End from the road to Saffron Walden

Gardens at North End

North End from outside North End Gatehouse

Kim, Paul, Emma and John

Back row: Paul, Paul, and John
Middle row: Kim, Trina and Emma
Front row: Ashley, Robert and Matthew

Kim

MR. & MRS. J. BASSETT

4 NORTH END

John, Kim, Paul and Emma

Kim was Cyril and Joyce Perrin's first of four children, followed by Kevin, Karen and Trina. She was born at 2 The Common with, as for the others, Nurse Clark in attendance. Kim is a person of enormous energy, she loves to be out and about, and works for Just Maids. John works at the Audley End Estate, painting and decorating. Paul who is 17, is in the first year of his 'A' level studies at the County High School. On the weekends he gardens at The Ice House next to the entrance of Audley End Park on Audley End road, and enterprisingly also earns pocket money cleaning at the new sports hall at the school. Emma is also at The County High, and is in her first year of GCSE study.

In the late fifties and early sixties the allotments behind Kim's home stretched up as far and were part of what is now the garden of The Old Telegraph House, which was then run by the Taylor family as a post office. Where Church Path and Church Walk are now there was a nettle field and some back gardens were made up into allotments and chickens kept.

Kim used to play with her best friend Jenny Starr, and her brother Bill, Betty Starr's children (not to be confused with Bill Starr who lives on Church Walk now), and Jeremy (Jumbo) Barker who lived at South House. In those days South House had a car park where Morlich Lodge now stands. They had an old pram, which Bill and Jumbo used to push Jenny around in but Kim recollects they once accidentally tipped her into the nettles.

In those days Flint Cottage, the one near the church, was two houses. Betty Starr lived in one side with her five children, Jean, Tony, Bill, Linda and Jenny. The other side was occupied by Arthur Davis who had a car. This was parked under the conker tree. The house next door was similarly divided; Miss Cork on one side and Jim Barnes, who had a dog called Betsy, on the other. Jim's house was forbidden to Kim and Jenny but the frequent litters of pups proved an irresistible attraction. Betsy's sweetheart was considered to be the Barker's terrier, Snowy. Whenever the Barkers arrived home after a trip Snowy would shoot up to Arthur Davis's car and back again, perhaps stopping off for love on the return!

Kim went to Littlebury School, she remembers being chased with the other children by a bulldog that was kept nearby, leaving the school grounds could be a terrifying experience !

Kim had always known John by acquaintance but met him properly at a disco in Clavering. They have lived at North End since 1982 and the whole family love it. Paul says that when he gets married he will move in with his bride and Kim and John will have to move out.

"The houses are out of the way but not too far, it's peaceful, the neighbours look out for each other taking in parcels or washing if it rains, we have good neighbours. "

recorder

MRS. P. ROMER

NORTH END FARM

Philippa

I am an artist, daughter of an artist, Hilda Kidman, and mother of an artist, Caroline Romer! I studied at the Royal Academy Schools in London and have been painting for many years, mainly portraits and especially portraits of children.

I moved from Braughing in Hertfordshire to North End Farm in September 1996, so I am a comparative newcomer to Littlebury. I had lived very happily in Braughing for forty years so it was particularly hard to move when the time came to sell my house there. However, luckily for me, after a long search, I found North End Farm tucked away across the river beyond the playing field, a little pink house with a barn and a lovely garden and a view to the north, right up the Cam Valley, perfect for my work. Until this year when Rectory Farm was sold, a flock of sheep grazed the water meadow and were a homely sight as they moved over the valley and came up to my garden fence in the evening. John Mclaren, son of Archie, told me that his family had always kept animals in the valley for the last seventy years and presumed that animals had grazed there for hundreds of years. So sadly in this year 2000, the valley feels empty without them.

Littlebury has a lovely church. I go to services there as regularly as I can and enjoy the social events, the Harvest Suppers, Epiphany party and the annual Church Fêtes. I also belong to 'Littlebury Ladies', a group who meet once a month for a talk and give newcomers a wonderful opportunity to meet other people who live in the village. Thank you Littlebury for giving me a very warm welcome - I am lucky and happy to be here.

a flock of sheep grazed the water meadow and were a homely sight as they moved over the valley and came up to my garden fence in the evening

Philippa paints fine portraits

North End Gatehouse

The Gatehouse from within its garden

The Walden Road leading into Littlebury

Mill Cottage

Back over the bridge

Looking up Mill Lane

Max and Gillian on their
Wedding Day

Riverside in the summer

MR. & MRS. MAX MCGREGOR

RIVERSIDE COTTAGE

Max and Gillian

Dearest Lizzie:

You would be quite within your rights never to speak to me again for failing to provide you with a short run-down on my miserable existence but I have now put you at the top of the priority list in sheer desperation and guilt. I would describe myself in the following way. "Born in New Zealand in 1921. After an education in NZ state schools where he managed to avoid all attempts to improve his reasoning ability with other than a basic understanding of the three R's during an idyllic childhood which seemed all sunshine, he succeeded in avoiding further attention by the education authorities by joining the RNZAF and deserting to England in 1940. Here he was even less successful at avoiding trouble (and work) by getting shot down in 1944, thus attracting to himself at a later date the unwanted attention of the German authorities by becoming their unwilling guest. The food and lodgings, though free, were not of an acceptable standard, so they parted willingly if not amicably in 1945. The NZ authorities now thought themselves entitled to an accounting for his protracted absence and as they were becoming importunate by insisting on his return, he deserted to Palestine. Here the sunshine really returned and he obtained for himself a built in servant by marrying a WRAF officer called Margot. After nineteen years happily spent with his family in various places around the world now annoying the RAF authorities and avoiding work as was his natural inclination he decided he could best avoid their demands for a quid pro quo by hiding in Littlebury in 1967. There, at least his wife found a degree of acceptance among the locals and he could continue his bent for indolence by basking in the resulting limelight. Unfortunately this pleasant life was rudely interrupted in 1998 by the usual mixture of illness and age resulting in the loss of Margot. But with his usual good luck in keeping out of trouble he managed to find another willing partner in the year 2000 in the shape of his late wife's 1947 bridesmaid, Gillian Dawson, who at the time of going to press seems just as capable as her predecessor in keeping him in a state of euphoria. This enables him to continue the saga of a man gifted in avoiding trouble, work and responsibility for the foreseeable future."

I hope this gets me off the hook, Love Max

Max's uniform worn at the 1995 VJ Day 50 year anniversary celebrations in the village still fitted him, that is what could be seen of it for medals. He met Margot while they were both stationed in Jerusalem and they were married in St George's Cathedral in 1947. He took early retirement from the RAF when a Wing Commander and subsequently worked in industry, moving to Littlebury with Margot and their children David and Judith, soon becoming very much involved in the life of the church and the community. He excels as an organist and also acts as choir master for Great Chesterford choir. Max has been a churchwarden and currently serves on the Village Hall Committee. Margot was a talented embroiderer, super cook, and a flower arranger for the church.

Gillian's career has been in the field of ballet where she became a recognised teacher and examiner both in the UK and abroad, never marrying, always retaining links with the inhabitants of Riverside. On August 12th 2000 bridesmaid and widower closed the 53 year gap in their individual histories by marrying under special licence in All Saints Church, Great Chesterford, thereby placing Riverside Cottage under new and happy management.

THE MCCAFFFREY FAMILY

LITTLEBURY MILLS (MODERN DAY MILLERS!)

Nick, Frances, Harriet 9, James 6, Katie 4.

We purchased the house and mill in 1999. Listed in the Domesday Book and once the private residence of the Dowager the late Lady Dorothy Braybrooke. Run down and dilapidated surrounded by water and on occasions partly filled with water! We have embarked on restoring the property into a family home.

The Mill

My name is Harriet. I am 9 years old. My favourite hobby is football. I have a brother called James and a sister called Katie. I like living here because it is fun and there is lots of garden to play in and I can play with our dog, Max - I like feeding the pig with daddy and I like watching Max do his dog training in the meadow. We see lots of birds in our garden. Sometimes we might see a heron on the island or in the Mill pool. These are some of the birds we see in our garden: Heron, Kingfisher, Cormorant, Moorhen and duck. Me, daddy and James do a lot of fishing we see lots of fish in the river. These are some of the fish we usually see in the river: Trout, Pike, Carp and Perch. Me and daddy canoe down the river in the summertime. Once our friend from America came to visit and him and me went right down the river to the gate and sometimes the bottom of the canoe got stuck on the stones at the Bottom of the riverbed but we managed to get it of the stones. One night I was watching a film. James and Katie were watching the film with me when I started shouting, "LOOK IT'S A BABY VOLE!" Because it looked like one. But I was wrong. James went to get daddy and he said that it was a Shrew. We found another 7 and one dead on the carpet. We have lots of pets. Our biggest one is a pig called Wilma. We have 4 chickens. We used to have 7 but our dog, Max killed one and one died of an illness and one went missing. We think a fox killed it. Last of all, our dog Max. He loves to run around through the woods and gardens. Joined to the side of our house is an island. We have a swing there. Sometimes it gets completely covered with water. This happens if we have a lot of rain and the river rises. I have a motor bike which I like to ride through our woods. In the mill there is a big wheel which in the olden days used to turn by the power of the water gushing through. The millstones are made of stone. They are very big and very heavy. They used to grind the wheat down into flour. There has been a lot of rain and floods recently. The river burst its banks and it covered the whole island the garden and the lane. The water got into the cellars and we had to call the fire brigade. The firemen pumped all the water out. It took all day.

My name is Katie I am 4 years old. I like playing in the garden. I like having picnics there and playing camps in the woods. I like feeding Wilma our pig and collecting the eggs from the chickens. I like my bedroom. It is very sunny. One day a lady came to visit us. She was very old and she said that she lived here for two years, during the war. It was a bed and breakfast then. She used to sleep in my room with her little baby while her husband was away.

My name is James I am 6 years old. I like the river. I go fishing with my daddy. I have got my own rod. I have caught a trout and a perch. I like feeding the fish from the downstairs toilet window. You can look down into the water and see all the fish swimming about and jumping up for the bread. Sometimes we see the kingfisher. He is bright blue and very secretive. We hear him first. He sounds like a squeaky old wheelbarrow. I like going into the mill to see the old wheel. I like living here.

The Mill House seen from the top of Mill Lane. It is the subject of the village sign

Frances, Katie, Harriet, Nick and James

'Wilma' a Tamworth pig with Nick

Inside the mill

The river millpond and sill

The river running quietly through Mill House garden the day before the flood

Mill Lane and its junction with Walden Road

A view of Riverside Cottage from The Mill House. The river flows through The Mill House garden from Audley End

Flooding in Mill Lane outside Mill Cottage in November

Gordon

Gordon in his beautiful
garden

MR. G. WILBY

THE OLD BAKERY

Gordon

I married in Newport in 1949 and with my wife Sheila we started our married life in the Old Bakery shop in Littlebury.

The people of Littlebury were so helpful and kind, not only were they our customers, but friends.

With many others, including dear Eric Bass, Sheila and I helped start the Littlebury recreation fund. The meetings used to be held in our house, when we all used to pay one shilling to get it off the ground.

In 1969 we moved to our new shop. There were so many lovely characters in the village, it was a pleasure for us to see them in the shop for a laugh and a joke.

When decimalization came in 1971 the Post Office shop closed, so we decided to take on the Post Office in our shop. The mail used to be delivered at 5.30 a.m. and the Post lady, Masie Webb used to sort the mail then deliver on foot to all the village.

Sheila and I had two children, Terry and Susan, Terry starting his school life at Littlebury. We retired in 1986 having seen so many changes in the past 37 years. The village gave us such a wonderful surprise party in the village hall, that we shall never forget.

Sadly, as with so many friends, Sheila died in September 1998 with wonderful memories of our life in Littlebury.

Gordon was treasurer of the Littlebury recreation fund. He is still a trustee of the village hall, also Chairman of the Royal British Legion.

Sheila

MRS. C. LAWRENCE

MULBERRY COTTAGE

WALDEN ROAD,

LITTLEBURY,

SAFFRON WALDEN,

Cynthia

On viewing Mulberry Cottage I immediately fell in love with the house, which is thatched, something I've probably always wanted, also the garden which is a delight, even with a small wood containing mostly yew trees also acacia and a plane tree which is the largest plane tree in Essex and of course a mulberry tree!

Littlebury is a lovely friendly village and we chose it because it then had a village shop, it was not far from Addenbrookes and Saffron Walden. We had retired when we came here in 1998, since then I have joined the National Association of Decorative and Fine Arts Society, also an Art group in Saffron Walden.

I really love having dinner parties; wanting to do something different I decided to bring a rather large table down from the garage, dragging it over the lawn which made great grooves. Getting to the kitchen door, no way could I get it into the kitchen, forgetting my husband had put castors on it, so upright, on its side, I struggled but how upset I got! The postman arrived, how lucky we are, what a wonderful man, there stood me and he said "Oh, can I help you?" Eventually getting into the kitchen, the pine unit I decided to put into the conservatory all decorated with candles was not large enough for the amount of people! So all the effort was to no avail and the table taken back the next day!

...even with a small wood containing mostly yew trees also acacia and a plane tree which is the largest plane tree in Essex and of course a mulberry tree!

Cynthia

This garden was the venue
for the children's tea on the
day of the VJ day
commemorative celebrations

'Bunty' and Roy with
Jean Cowell

MR. AND MRS. R. AGER

5 CHURCH WALK

Roy and Betty (Bunty) with Jean Cowell, Betty's sister (10 Merton Place)

Roy worked for 41 years at Abbey Farm, and at the time he was made redundant applied for and was allocated a council house. Their connections in Littlebury are long standing; Betty's grandmother lived on the Common, (which is now called Church Walk) and Betty sang, occasionally solo, in Littlebury Church Choir. She and Shirley Marsh also sang when there were social evenings held in the Village Hall in the '50s, at which time Betty lived at 10 Merton Place.

Roy and Betty were married on September 22nd 1956 at Littlebury Church.

recorder

MR. & MRS. L. GREEN

6 CHURCH WALK

Les and Hilda

Hilda comes from Stamford Hill where her father was the local undertaker. She worked in haute couture just before the war, a fact which told against her with the onset of conscription as it was a luxury trade. She was drafted into the Greenford Ordnance Stores which was constantly targeted by the Germans.

Hilda was married, and had two children but sadly the marrriage ended. Les and Hilda met in 1966 (Les says 1066). They lived in a mobile home at Takely near Stansted. After the noise of the war they loved the peace and quiet of the country, but as the airport expanded they were moved to make way for the station and applied for Council accommodation and came to Littlebury, finally making their home their own in 1994. Les and Hilda have made many improvements, the house is light and airy.

Les comes from Hackney. He joined the army in 1941 when only 16, lying about his age. He was involved in the Normandy Landings and a shell damaged his eyes and land mines affected his ears at Caen. He was discharged in 1945 after a series of medicals. Les applied to train in horticulture but his eye problems persisted. After several operations special glasses enabled him to see and work. After training he worked for the L.C.C. as it was then known and ended up as Head Gardener for the Waterboard.

The garden is testament to a lifetime's knowledge, and Les has been known to advise a grateful recorder on pruning.

recorder

Les has green fingers

Les and Hilda

The apple trees are pruned
bi-annually

Bill

MR. W. STARR

10 CHURCH WALK

Bill

Bill first came to live at Littlebury in 1927 when he was six. He and his family moved into Mill Cottage with his grandmother after his father died. He recollects that the very night they moved in there was a huge fire at the chaff factory in Peggy's Walk. The fire engine was parked between Mill Cottage and the Mill; the water pumped up to the main road and then pumped again to Peggy's Walk. Bill attended Littlebury School when Mrs Clay was the headmistress.

He was apprenticed to Thurgood's Garage at Chesterford and when it was sold, worked at the petrol station at Stump Cross. When that was sold, Bill left and went to work at Engelman's Nursery until he was called up. Enlisted in the 6th Armoured Division he went to North Africa; Algeria and Tunisia. They met up with the 8th Army and Bill finished his war in Italy.

Returning to Littlebury in 1946, Bill had his own family business, a wood round and a smallholding. He recollects that during the '50s there were two shops, one called Mellors in what is now The Little House opposite the pub, and one which was also a Post Office. There was a Bakery, a Blacksmith (in the thatched cottage opposite Rectory Close), a Wheelwright, and three Public Houses.

Bill worked at Mclaren's Farm from about 1958, until he retired. During his retirement Bill gardened at The Queen's Head, and North and South Houses. Bill plays bowls in the village hall with the Bowls Club as his main recreation, he will be 80 next March.

Until recently Bill has produced vegetables in his own garden, but now tends just his flowers. Dahlias, chrysanthemums, roses, dianthus and many others delight passers-by.

recorder

MR. B. M. AUGER

"EVA'S" CHURCHWALK,

Barry

Barry was born in the village on 17th December 1941, son of Eva and George Auger. We lived at Flint Cottage, Mill Lane with my grandparents William and Alice Dew who ran the local newspaper round. Grandad Dew delivered the newspapers seven days a week to the whole of Littlebury, Audley End, Littlebury Green, Catmere End and Strethall on his trade bike.

I now live in Church Walk with my partner and friend Charlie F. Williams where we run our own Painting, Decorating, House sitting service and Gardening business. I am also the local Uttlesford Carer and village Caretaker.

Barry and Charlie

Freddie, Nicola and Anthony

DR. & MRS. A. COLCLOUGH

FLINT COTTAGE

Anthony, Nicola and Freddie

Nicola and Anthony moved into Flint Cottage in April 1999. Prior to that they lived in Chertsey, Surrey where they had gone after finishing University in Guildford.

Nicola, who is originally from Saffron Walden, read Chemistry at University and then went on to complete a PhD. She joined Coopers & Lybrand in 1994 and now works in the Cambridge office of Pricehouse Coopers.

Anthony, who is originally from Swansea in South Wales, read Materials Science as a first degree and also completed a PhD. He has worked in the City since 1993 and joined a Lloyds Syndicate as a Credit and Political Risk underwriter in 1997. Very recently, November 2000, he moved to Sirius International Insurance Company.

Both Anthony and Nicola have always played all sports and met through the hockey club at University. Anthony still plays hockey, both locally for Bishops Stortford, and at international level for Wales. Amongst other achievements he won a gold medal playing for Great Britain Students in the World Student Games in Kuala Lumpur, Malaysia in 1998, as well as winning several national titles with Teddington Hockey Club.

Anthony has over 100 senior caps for Wales and two for Great Britain which he won when in the final squad of 25 players training for the Atlanta Olympics in 1996. Unfortunately he missed selection for the final squad of 16. Anthony and Nicola also enjoy golf and Anthony is a member of Saffron Walden Golf Club.

A new addition to the family arrived in October. Frederick James was born at 7.44 pm on Monday 30th October in the Rosie at Addenbrookes Hospital. He weighed 5lb 15oz and is feeding and sleeping well. Freddie has totally taken over his parents' lives and added to the enjoyment of living in Littlebury.

MR. & MRS. K. WINTER

LIME TREE COTTAGE

Keith, Gabbie and Cara

Gabrielle and I fell in love with Lime Tree Cottage the minute we stepped out into the rear garden and saw the church rising above the ivy covered wall, framed in part by the huge lime tree. We were living at that time in Stansted Mountfitchet. The house was large, but modern and although we weren't actually looking to move, we didn't feel completely settled. By chance we saw the cottage in the local paper and were tempted to take a look. I didn't realise until we arrived to view, that I already had a connection with the house.

It had once belonged to George and Di Barker, well known Littlebury residents, whose son Jeremy (or Jumbo as he is known) was a friend of mine and a fellow musician. I had been in the village on a number of occasions when I was younger but could remember very little as it was normally late at night, following a gig in Cambridge that I would find myself stopping here briefly on my way back home to Bishops Stortford.

Lime Tree Cottage was created out of two old dwellings purchased from Audley End (for the sum of £400 I believe!). It had been much altered and extended by the Swains from whom we purchased it and here we are, fifteen years on still enjoying the atmosphere created by the lime tree and that view of the church.

Our daughter Cara arrived six months after we moved in. Were it not for the timely advice to get going that we received from our friend, neighbour and local midwife June Michin she would, almost certainly, have been born in Littlebury itself. We made it to the Rosie just in time!!

Cara attended the primary school in Great Chesterford and is now studying (hard we hope!) at Newport where her great love is hockey! Sorry Cara, you can't do it for GCSE!!

A lasting memory for us, thinking back to our first days as residents here, will always be the friendly welcome we received when we first moved in. We have also come to appreciate Saffron Walden's quintessential market town atmosphere and feel very much that we are fortunate indeed to live where we do. During my time at Newport Grammar School as a very average schoolboy I did have occasion to visit the town with friends and felt even then that it was somehow just that little bit special. Despite these ever more rapidly changing times we certainly feel that Saffron Walden and indeed Littlebury itself has retained much that is to be treasured.

Cara wrote: I was born on the 13th (lucky for some!) January 1986! I am 14 years old now, and I am a student at Newport Free Grammar School. I am a keen hockey player, in school and out. I play for my school team, Saffron Walden Ladies, and last year I played for the Cambridge county team.

I am very into music, which is one of the reasons why I chose Newport as a secondary school (as well as their tuck shop!!). I play the piano, sax and guitar and write and sing my own songs, which is what I would love to do when I'm older! The type of music that I am into is Indie/rock! My favourite band and artists are Sting, Imogen Heap, Stereophonics, Alanis Morisette, Ricki Lee Jones and O2!

My favourite subjects at school are the expressive and creative ones, ie. Art, Music, Drama, English and Graphic Products! I also enjoy learning Italian, for I find it a nice language to be able to speak!

Keith, Cara and Gabbie

The view from the back garden

Nurse

NURSE CLARK

13 CHURCH WALK

'Nurse'

'Nurse', as she is still affectionately known, was born in 1906. She came to Littlebury as a District Nurse and Midwife a year before the war and then, when war was declared, as part of the reserved occupation in 1939. Coming from Ilford in the suburbs of London where there were indoor flush toilets, gas lighting and running water to having to use standpipes and the night soil van in Littlebury Green (as in all the villages around) was very different from what she was used to. In her first year the parish was very peaceful.

'Nurse' along with the farmer, the doctor and the vicar were allowed vehicles, and she had to learn to drive, being taught by Raynhams Garage (three lessons), and practising with the young women who held licences and didn't work, coming as they did from the better off families. She had a two seater Morris and drove at night with only the sidelights on, half blacked out, which was all that was permitted, leaning out of the window to see more clearly. Sometimes coming home from Chrishall Nurse missed the turning unable to see the sign post. Her petrol allowance was only for work, Nurse adhered strictly to this, often walking with friends into Walden.

Food was rationed, there was one egg a week, and one third of a pint of milk a day. On one occasion a person in Littlebury Green gave her a Kilner jar of fresh cow's milk. It had not been cooled and by the time she arrived home had turned solid. It was thrown away, but Nurse says that now she knows it could have been used for scones! Another time the Medical Oficer was called to inspect the water from the well at North End which was found to have 'whirley things' in it. The evacuees there were told that there was no danger in drinking it as there was no human effluent running in the nearby water courses, and that if they were anxious, to walk half a mile (with their buckets) to the standpipe in Littlebury! Nurse says that it is a good thing that nowadays we have antibiotics.

The District nurses from Chesterford and Newport were her friends and they all helped each other out when needed. Only 'emergency' babies were delivered at hospital, beds being reserved for casualties.

Nurse Clark recollects that there was a good bus service, two village shops, a sweet shop, three pubs in Littlebury and two at Littlebury Green. People were very friendly. At this time there were many evacuees and they were billeted in Army huts. In a hut constructed by the Army (where the Village Hall now stands) there were whist drives. Some of the village girls married the soldiers. One of the evacuees told Nurse that she and others with children were bundled into lorries, and evacuated out of London without they or their husbands being told where they were going. Ammunition was stored in lanes leading to Littlebury Green and Chestnut Avenue, there were Pineys ('Pineapples' which were hand grenades) and 'Remmies'. The Somersets were at Chesterford and some of those girls married the soldiers also. Nurse's sister (she was one of six children) was married on Battle of Britain Day. She and her husband stayed with Nurse in her three rooms at St. John' s Cottage on their honeymoon. Nurse says she worked for thirty years without a day off for sickness. Her legs are not so good now, Jane Appleby takes her shopping, and with the trolley she can manage well. She says that she has had interesting work. She is often to be seen at village and church occasions. Nurse says she is mentally 'fair'. Something of an understatement.

recorder

REV. LAWRENCE BOND & MRS. DAWN BOND

THE VICARAGE

LITTTLEBURY

Dawn, Laurie, Cheryl and Simon

Dawn & Laurie came to Littlebury on the 21st December 1995 and, sadly for the village, left on 21st March 2000. In between they became a very popular and valued part of village life.

The shop and post office had been closed for 18 months and Dawn opened a part time post office on Monday and Thursday mornings, which was much appreciated. Dawn worked as a cook at St. Mark's College and looked after the rota for the Sunday School teachers. Laurie, in addition to his pastoral duties was very involved in Uttlesford Community Travel, The Stort Valley Schools Trust, and was a governor for Great Chesterford School. He is very keen on cricket, and he and Dawn both enjoy a keen interest in gardening and line dancing.

Dawn was often to be found putting the finishing touches to a line dancing skirt when in between customers in her conservatory post office, which also became a meeting place for villagers. The approach to it was through a special grass and lavender planted gravel garden. It was always a particular pleasure to send parcels, or buy stamps surrounded by exotic plants and cacti, and be able to look through to the back garden which boasted, among other things, fruit cages and a hosta lined Lakeland stream which ran down the side of a particularly well kept lawn. The last session was held a few days before their move to Takeley and Little Canfield.

On the 17th February Laurie and Dawn were jointly awarded an Uttlesford District Community Award for which they had been recommended by the Parish Council. Their farewell service in the church on 19th February was followed by a buffet lunch in the village hall, with everybody who came bringing a dish. It was a cheerful occasion but with an underlying sense of impending loss.

Laurie writes: " We are now happily settled in Takeley and I am looking after the parishes of Takeley and Little Canfield. They are two very different villages, but both have their own special character. Little Canfield only has 300 residents, who are scatttered along about 5 miles of the A120. Takeley has 3,500 residents, but these are grouped around 5 or 6 different centres of population. We have quickly settled into life in the community here, but there was already a post office, so Dawn has been let off that one. Instead she cooks at Takeley Day Centre, cleans at Takeley Primary School and also runs a linedance there. She is stiill working at St. Mark's College and has also been recruited as a cook at Saffron Walden Day Centre!"

As things are Laurie will be the last incumbent vicar in Littlebury. There is a possibility that a non-stipendiary minister may be allowed to live in the house, but there are no guarantees.

recorder

Laurie and Dawn in the 'Post Office'.

The 'Lakeland' Stream

A gift for Laurie and Dawn
from Littlebury presented by
Alastair Lloyd

John Penney, Ruth Rigby,
Max McGregor, Elspeth
Grant, Denis Wright and Jon
Wayper

Laurie's leaving speech

Lower Church Walk, west facing

Upper Church Walk from outside Flint Cottage

The Vicarage is on the right and 'Eva's' garden is in the foreground, 2 The Common is in the distance on the right

Mollie and Laurie

MR. & MRS. L. WARD

CAMBRAE COTTAGE

Laurie and Mollie

Laurie and Mollie married in 1949. They moved from Harrogate to Littlebury in 1989 to be near their younger daughter and her family.

Laurie is a retired Corporate Planning Manager and Mollie a retired Civil Servant. Both are members of the District Church Council and Laurie, a former Church Warden, is a member of the Deanery Synod. He is also a founder member of the Saffron Walden Archive Society.

Mollie is a member, and former Chairperson of Littlebury Ladies and helps with flower arranging in the Church this being one of her special interests.

JOHN AND SHIRLEY TIPTON AND JEAN SMITH,

RODING HOUSE,

CHURCH WALK,

LITTLEBURY.

We moved to Church Walk in September 1987, the month before the "Big Storm" hit the village and put the lights out for a week. "So this is country living," we thought. Our arrival was watched with interest by the neighbours - I was obviously not dressed in my smartest attire for moving house and Joyce Perrin thought I was one of the removal men. Hello, Littlebury.

We had both just retired from teaching in Harlow, so migration to a rural environment was certain to be beneficial: and so it worked out. But it was not to be an idle existence. Before long Shirley had been persuaded to become Treasurer of the Village Hall Committee, so we had become a part of the village community.

I was soon persuaded to become Chairman of Littlebury Football Club and later, when Littlebury Carpet Bowls Club was formed, I was Chairman of that too. (Chairman is a good job - you do very little but tell others what to do.)
A large slice of our leisure time is devoted to Radwinter Bowls Club, of which Shirley is Treasurer. We also play a lot of Bridge and I play golf - badly! The cinema and the theatre too are on the agenda. The cliché about wondering how we ever found time to go to work certainly applies to us.

Most important to us though, are our friends and family. We welcomed the new millennium with our closest friends at a special House Party at Roding House. At Midnight as the Church bells rang out we celebrated the arrival of the new millennium with fireworks. It was one of those defining moments; the sky above Littlebury played host to a galaxy of colour as each rocket and roman candle screeched upwards before showering its stars and sprays of light. All around the village families and friends were doing the same.

The other member of our household, Shirley's mother Jean, came to live with us three years ago and celebrated her ninetieth birthday in August. She is a sprightly nonagenarian, who enjoys reading and keeping her hand in with the duster and the iron. She is an expert at cleaning the family silver, having spent the years before her marriage in service. Her tales of growing up in a large, but poor family in Edwardian England highlight how much has changed during the century.

Shirley, John and Jean

Millennium Celebrations in
the Tipton household

Joyce and Cyril

The garden is very productive

CYRIL AND JOYCE PERRIN

Cyril was born at 4 Baker's Row, Littlebury and has lived in the village all his life. A year after he married Joyce, who came from Radwinter, they moved into their cottage in Church Walk. The cottage answers to the name of The White Cottage or 2 The Common, though it's not white and there is no common any more.

Their four children, Kim, Kevin, Karen and Katrina and their seven grandchildren all still live in the village. Cyril was a keen cricketer with the village club and a founder member, back in the sixties, of Littlebury Football Club.

He has worked in agriculture since he left the village school and has been at Kent's Farm and Home Farm for the last thirty-five years. The residents of Church Walk set their clocks by the sound of Cyril's tractor returning home for lunch.

John Tipton

MRS. S. THOMAS

14 CHURCH WALK

Sheila

In 1966 Sheila moved to Littlebury as a young widow with three children under the age of five. She drove a 66 old Ford with side indicators. Sheila chose Littlebury because it had two bus services, Premier and Eastern Counties No 112. There was a shop, a Post Office and a pub and most important, a school. The school closed in 1968 and there had to be a bus to take all the children to Great Chesterford who definitely gave preference to Great Chesterford children.

There was a very high profile village life with Amateur Dramatics, Ladies British Legion and an almost weekly dance. This was so popular that entry was limited to between 90-120 people. It was often over subscribed. Lady Braybrooke who gave the village its hall, used to hold the Church fête, complete with a children's Fancy Dress. There was flooding in the late '60s and early '70s and in 1976 a lorry drove into one of the houses in the Walden Road. Sheila helped with the Littlebury 'Lympics, a yearly event lasting one week, starting with a sponsored walk (Sheila was one of the first to walk on the as yet unpainted M11), it included indoor and outdoor games ending on Saturday with a Boat Race, and a barbecue and dance in the evening.

The year 2000. No bus, No shop, No school, No vicar - is this progress ?

Sheila and many others were newcomers to Littlebury in the 1960s and they got together and revived the social life of the village. She was a very active member of the Granta Players, and has a wonderful collection of photograhs of many of the productions given in the village hall, one of which is reproduced here. She remembers when the shop would deliver if you left an order in the shop, and that there were bands for the dances because the village could afford them. Because of the shop and these activities, people would meet up. Now she feels that people don't speak and are even suprised if you pass the time of day on the street. Commuters live in the village and are not interested in village life. Sheila was made redundant in 1996, she took on a job for a while, working two mornings a week, but since she retired finds life much more enjoyable. A passionate Bridge player, she plays at Hadstock, is a member of the Second Littlebury Carpet Bowls team, and with her daughters and grandson all living quite close Sheila has as busy a life as she ever did.

Sheila

Not many sheds have a bay window

Heading west on the Walden Road from the drive of the Village Hall

Looking towards Church Walk along Church Path

High Street. The Old Telegraph House on the left and Parrishes on the right in the foreground with The Gate House in the distance

The Mobile library comes
every Thursday afternoon

The Post bus

From the 'Triangle' towards
the Walden Road. Kents
Farmhouse was having its
front door replaced after a
car ran into it

Minna, Matias, Milja and
Heikki

Minna with 'Konsta'

HEIKKI, MINNA, MILJA AND MATIAS LEHVASLAIHO
OLD NO. 3,
HIGH STREET

Four and a half years ago we toured Europe for two weeks by car. Our starting point was Finland, our native country. We visited eight countries and ended up staying in Littlebury for a couple of days with friends who had temporarily rented a cottage in the village. I immediately fell in love with the area and thought that Littlebury was the loveliest village I had ever seen. To cut a long story short: three months later we were back in Littlebury but this time buying a house, and Heikki had started to work at the Genome Campus in Hinxton. A few months later, after we had settled down, also I started to work at the campus. We both work in the field of bioinformatics.

In our spare time Heikki enjoys taking photographs and going for long walks with our dogs. I am a member of the Littlebury Recreation committee, and I am also one of the 'Owls' in the 1st Littlebury Brownies pack that meets weekly in the village hall. I have also immensely enjoyed being a bell-ringer in our church and doing face painting in different fund raising events in and around the village.

Our daughter Milja (12 years old) is a devoted skier. She also loves to play the piano, and to listen to pop-music, so we travel down to London for concerts quite often. She enjoys being with her friends and watching scary movies with them. She also enjoys our animal collection: two dogs, a pig, terrapins and a tortoise.

Our son Matias (5 years old) enjoys wall climbing, scootering and studying dinosaurs. His favourite place to visit is the Natural History Museum in London, so we know it nearly as well as our own village by now. He also likes to watch nature programmes on TV, such as those of an Australian crocodile hunter. He is very impressed with his two commercial pilot uncles, and plans to combine his two loves and become a flying palaeontologist when he grows up. He has already started his career by helping for a day at the Saffron Walden Museum dinosaur exhibition.

Minna

```
                              ^..^
                              (oo)
===|====|====|====|====|====|====|====|====|====|====|=w==w====|
Minna Lehvaslaiho  = SWISS-PROT Database Curator   ~( :: )  |
European Bioinformatics Institute EMBL-EBI          w  w   |
Wellcome Trust Genome Campus        Phone +44(0)1223 494461 |
Cambridge CB10 1SD, United Kingd    Fax   +44(0)1223 494468 |
===|====|====|====|====|====|====|====|====|====|====|====|====|
```

THE QUEEN'S HEAD
HIGH STREET

PROPRIETOR: MR. M. HOUSDEN, WITH THE ASSISTANCE OF MR. D. CAMMANN
Martin and David

Martin came to The Queen's Head on 6th November. He has lived in Saffron Walden all his life and he knew the pub as a local and a customer. Five years ago he expressed an interest in it and has now managed to take on a tenancy through Greene King.

The Queen's Head was once a 16th Century Inn and house, until about thirteen years ago when Jeremy and Debbie O'Gorman bought it, knocked the two together and completely refurbished it. Since they left there have been an assortment of managers running The Queen's Head with varying degrees of success.

Martin and David are making a positive effort to breathe new life into The Queen's Head taking care to serve good ales and quality fare. In between opening hours there is a continuing programme of refurbishment. There are no fruit machines or jukeboxes, just a relaxed and friendly atmosphere (with maybe a little light background jazz!).

David says there is only one pub in the village (where once there were three) and it is important to maintain The Queen's Head as a vibrant focal point for the locals as well as creating a destination for those coming from further afield. Although a licensed premises, local people come, and ladies meet for lunch and coffee in front of the fire.

Martin and David are interested in researching the history of the pub and its association with the village and are keen to obtain any information whether it be pictures, photos, memorabilia or even anecdotal stories. 'Shimmy' (Roy Seaman), a long term resident of Littlebury has much to tell. He remembers how the garden was a fuel dump during the war, and how, when the M11 was being built nearby the workmen became good customers and The Queen's Head found itself painted 'Wimpey' yellow!

Martin is delighted that already, after only six weeks in the village people have been congratulating him on returning The Queen's Head to a comfortable country inn feel.

The Queen's Head opens all day on Fridays and Saturdays
From 12.00-3.00pm and 5.30-11.00pm on weekdays
From 12.00-3.00pm and 7.00-10.30pm on Sundays

Cheers!

recorder

Martin in the kitchen

David in the bar

'Girls' from the village enjoy a celebratory opening night at their local

Karl Llewellyn, local Community Policeman in the car park of The Queen's Head

Leaving The Queen's Head

Milk delivered by Walden Dairy between five and six o'clock in the morning

Papers are deilvered daily

Our Postman, John

An oil delivery

Rubbish is both disposed of

and recycled

The High Street, Mill Cottage, Squirrels and The Long House looking south

The Old School House under snow at the beginning of the year

Granta House, The Old School House, and a glimpse of High House looking north

The Old Coach House with part of what was once the Parish or Reading Room in the foreground

James, Janice and Graham

James and Patches in the garden

THE WATSON FAMILY

THE OLD COACH HOUSE

We have lived in Littlebury since April 1988. We had contracted to buy our house the previous autumn when the house was a roofless ruin with a garden so overgrown it was impossible to walk through. The builders started work on the renovation of the house (which was formerly the coach house to the original Littlebury vicarage - now South House and North House) and a modern rear extension immediately after the famous gales of October 1987. We, as a family, were to be seen in the village most weekends checking on progress, and taking some memorable photographs, until we were finally able to move in during April 1988.

About ten years ago we bought from the Church the building on the road frontage. This was formerly the Littlebury Reading Room or Parish Room. We understand that it was built in Victorian times by a vicar of Littlebury as a playroom for his children. Over the years it has had many uses including a dining room where the children from the village school had their lunches, a scout hut and most recently as a centre for sorting newspapers before delivery. After we refurbished the building it has been used as a garage.

We are a small family, Graham and Janice Watson, and our seventeen-year-old son James.

Graham has been very active within the village over the years we have been residents. Initially he joined the Recreation Committee and was soon persuaded to join the Village Hall Committee where he was responsible for setting up its charitable status. He was asked to put his name forward for the Parish Council and served for several years, including two years as chairman. Since 1993 he has served as Churchwarden and during that time helped to set up, and then register as a charity, the Friends of Littlebury Church. He is also a trustee of The Jane Bradbury Educational Trust and the chairman of the Littlebury branch of the Saffron Walden Constituency Conservative Association.

Janice has just completed three years as treasurer of Littlebury Village Hall. James is a student in his upper sixth year at The Perse School in Cambridge and hopes to gain a place at university to study Classics. We have a family pet, Patches. who is a collie-cross rescue dog which we got from Wood Green Animal Shelter in August 1991.

We remember participating as a family in many events over the years, from Beetle Drives, village clean-ups, church lunches and suppers, to the V.E. and V.J. celebrations in 1995.

DR. & MRS. B. SANDERS

NORTH HOUSE

Brian (Sandy), Lizzie and Guy

Sandy

In 1940, at the age of three, Sandy was evacuated from the London Blitz to Saffron Walden. He then lived in Bridge House at Bridge End until he was eight, attending South Road and The Boys' British Schools. He became a choirboy at St Mary's Church when he was six. Following D. Day (which he clearly remembers as it was his seventh birthday) and the end of the war the following year, he returned to London when his father came home after serving abroad for five years with the Eighth Army.

Missing Walden greatly, his parents allowed him to return every school holiday to his adoptive parents the Tredgetts. He was allowed to roam the countryside freely and learned to fish on the River Cam between Littlebury and the Chesterfords. As he grew older he earned pocket money working on local farms, picking peas and potatoes and driving the tractor at harvest time.

Returning to live at North House Littlebury with Lizzie in 1987 they continue to do so happily ever after with their son Guy born in 1990. Both Lizzie and Sandy are artists and their studio overlooks the garden. Bliss.

Sandy still fishes the Cam as a member of the Audley Fly Fishing Club. On his first evening on the river the season after coming to the village, a Spitfire and a Hurricane flew above him following the river and he thought himself returned to childhood before realizing that they were from Duxford Museum.

Lizzie

We bought North House on a whim and have never regretted it. Londoners as we were, Littlebury and Saffron Walden held sway not only because of their ancient beauty and excellent communications but because of Sandy's connections. Furthermore, North House also has two huge north east facing windows, ideal for artists (the sunlight is off the windows by lOam which for us is about perfect), and to our delight a much larger garden than we were used to. We gardened so enthusiastically that Mrs Lloyd kindly suggested we opened, alongside Granta House for the National Gardens Scheme, which we did for three years, it was a privilege and a breathtaking regime. We retired jointly with a mixture of regret and relief, the garden now has a visibly more relaxed feeling. It enjoys wonderful bird life; at breakfast we watch the antics of the finches, tits, robins, wrens, and tree creepers in the undergrowth under the trees at the front of the house. In the shooting season pheasants often take refuge in the back and mysteriously one summer, two peacocks favoured us for forty eight hours, waking us with their unearthly calls.

We have many good friends here, Littlebury is a sociable and welcoming place. Our son Guy, born ten weeks early, is now ten and goes to Gibson House School. Currently we are particularly proud of him as, through his school, he was given a 'Service before Self' award by the Saffron Walden branch of the Rotary Club (So, William Waldegrave, who gave the thumbs down to further funding for neonates !). Lizzie's daughter Jojo (also similarly premature, now Arts Correspondent on the Independent,) is shortly to have her second child, and she and her family are moving to the area from London. This year is Lizzie's second as a Parish Councillor. Compiling this album has given her the pleasure of meeting many more people in the parish and through Elspeth Grant she has just started reading for the S.W. Talking Newspaper.

Sandy, Guy and Lizzie

At the back of North House

Bobby, Nicholas, Alexander, Mark and Caroline just before the move to The Old Rectory

High summer in South House back garden

THE GOULDER FAMILY AT SOUTH HOUSE

We moved to South House thirteen years ago as a newly-wed couple. We chose Littlebury because we wanted to be near Cambridge for Caroline's music there and within reasonable travelling times for our work. To start with we both had jobs, Nick in London and Caroline teaching in Bishops Stortford. We loved South House from the beginning, although we had lots of work to do to renovate and redecorate it. The garden too had grown rather wild, and we worked hard to put it in order.

Then along came our three boys, Alexander (1989), Mark (1990), and Bobby (1994). South House became a real family home.

Gradually the garden became a football pitch, and the boys started to outgrow their rooms. So we wanted a larger home - but we didn't want to leave Littlebury. We were very lucky to be able to buy The Old Rectory at the end of last year.

That too has needed a huge overhaul, but we know we will be as happy there as we have been here - more space, but still in Littlebury.

Mark

I like doing the bottle stall at the fête. Moving into the new house is good because we can play tennis every day. I like Littlebury because it has a friendly atmosphere.

Alexander

I like living in Littlebury because the people are very friendly. I also like the church fête every year because you get to meet new people and children. I like our new house because my room is on the 3rd floor and it is lime green and navy blue.

Bobby

I like our new house because my carpet is one of my favourite colours.

THE BELL RINGERS

On Sundays, Christmas Eve and New Year's Eve, weddings and for other special occasions (for example, for Queen Elizabeth, the Queen Mother's 100th birthday in August) Holy Trinity Church bells ring. Approximately every other Thursday evening the bell ringers also turn out to practise. On the evening that these pictures were taken the following were present: (clockwise from the left), John Harvey from Wendens Ambo, Roy Seaman; Tower Master, Shirley Green, Frances Griffiths from Newport, Annette Jacobs from Duddenhoe End, Eddie Archer from Saffron Walden and David, Annette' s husband. Occasionally, when there is a shortage Jon and Liz Wayper will help out.

In the bell tower is displayed a certificate from The Essex Association of Change Ringers to say that on Saturday, lst January 2000 Roy Seaman, Shirley Green, Jon and Liz Wayper, David and Annette Jacob, Jeni Dodds, Nicola Hards, Rob Albon and Roland Webb rang the New Year in. The bellringers from the beginning of the last century are not forgotten either; beneath the certificate is held a treasured slate on which has been beautifully inscribed the names of those who rang that year in, and which bells they rang.

A peal of Bob Doubles was
rung on these bells from
11.45 to 12.15 on Dec 31st 1900-1901.
J. Perrin Treble   C. Kirby Fourth
W. Abraham Second   E. Linwood Fifth
A. Clay Third   C. Bass Tenor
C.C. Woodley

The bells are still known as 'treble', 'two', 'three', 'four', 'five' and 'tenor'. Some ringers favour certain of the bells though it is expected that they should be able to take any of them, with the exception of the tenor, which because of its weight is generally rung by a man. When not enough bell ringers are present, only chiming is possible, as opposed to ringing.

Sometimes not all the bell ringers are able to attend. On these occasions those present have sometimes been known to take two ropes and Roy to take three at once, one in each hand and a loop on one of his feet.

recorder

Roy and Shirley with the slate from a hundred years ago

The procession up Mill Lane
led by John Harvey

'Reveille' played by
John Hammond

"We shall remember them"

ROYAL BRITISH LEGION

The Littlebury branch of the Royal British Legion was formed in 1967 with 27 members. The officers then were - The Rev. John West (vicar of Littlebury); Chairman and Treasurer the late Cecil Woodley; Secretary Denis Wright. The present officers are - President Alastair Lloyd; Chairman Gordon Wilby, Vice chairman Derek Grinham; Treasurer Brian Sugden; Secretary Denis Wright. The membership is now 35.

Remembrance Sunday

Every year since 1967 the branch has paraded, with its standard, on Remembrance Sunday for a service of Remembrance and Dedication round the War Memorial (only once has bad weather prevented this) at which the names of the men and women from the village who died in the two world wars are read out; 24 in 1914-18, and 3 in 1939-45. In recent years we have been fortunate to have the presence of John Hammond to sound 'The Last Post' and 'Reveille' on his trumpet. The service is then continued in Church and is very well supported by members of the village.

Poppy Collection

Denis and Mary Wright have organised our Poppy Collection since 1967. The sum raised has increased each year and this year we expect to send £1,400 to the National Poppy Appeal. In later years other collectors have assisted.

Benevolence

The late Cecil Woodley left a handsome legacy to the branch for benevolent purposes. There is a Services Committee of five branch members who meet annually to decide how the accumulated interest on the capital (invested with the Charities Aid Foundation) should be dispensed. It goes to branch members and their dependants who are in need of help and to two Legion retirement / convalescent homes. This year the sum distributed will be £860.

Social

The branch organises an annual 'fish and chip' supper in the Village Hall. This is open to anyone who likes to come. Members of the branch take part in various Bowls competitions and have won several trophies.

There is at least one Jumble Sale each year to raise funds to cover branch expenses.
Alastair Lloyd

HOLY TRINITY CHURCH

Our church dates from the middle of the 12th century and in 1875 the Chancel was entirely rebuilt and the Tudor windows of the aisles and Clerestory replaced. There is not a large congregation but those who attend are loyal and regular. However, the Christingle service was packed to overflowing.

THE CHRISTINGLE SERVICE

Among the many services that are held in Holy Trinity Church during the course of the year, one of the most popular is The Christingle Service which is specially for the children. The Christmas carols heralding the celebration of Christ's birth combined with the delight of the lit candles on the symbolically (and deliciously!) decorated oranges appeals to young and old alike.

JANE BRADBURY'S EDUCATIONAL FOUNDATION

The Trustees of this foundation meet twice yearly to consider applications for awards from, or on behalf of, young persons under the age of twenty five years, resident in the parish of Littlebury. The awards are for educational purposes of all types, including vocational and further educational training, attendance at field and other courses, the purchase of tools, equipment, instruments, books and clothing.

The foundation has also given funds to the Recreation Committee for play equipment and regularly to Great Chesterford School and Saffron Walden County High School because children of the parish attend them.

The trustees currently are: Rev. Duncan Green, Mrs. Lloyd, chair, Mrs. Appleby, clerk, Mrs. Andrew, Mrs. Menell, Miss Elspeth Grant, Mrs. Penney, Mrs. Walsh, Mrs. Warren and Mr. Watson. There is a brass of Jane Bradbury near the font.

LITTLEBURY UNITED CHARITIES

In 1953 the 9th Lord Braybrooke, father of the current Lord Braybrooke, arranged with the Charity Commissioners that a new charity Scheme should be made by adapting the old parish half-crown charity. The Scheme, which covers the whole parish, is an amalgamation of several old parish charities using the best possible methods of giving. Initially £15.00 a year was put by for gifts of clothing for the most urgent cases. In 1999 £310.00 was given to parishioners, of which £30.00 went to residents of Littlebury Green, £20.00 to Catmere End and the rest in amounts of £12.00 or £20.00 to Littlebury. Mrs. Lloyd is Chairman and Mr. Wright Clerk, Secretary and Treasurer. The four other trustees are the Rev. Duncan Green, Miss Elspeth Grant, Mrs. Menell and Mrs. Penney.

Holy Trinity Church under snow

The children made a circle around the pews with their Christingle candles. For this service there was standing room only

Ellie Berisford. The sweets are often consumed by the end of the service!

Sonnet MM

Beneath the bridge the shady Granta glides,
This ancient crossing fixed the village site,
But gaudy signs pronounce its crumbling plight,
Our rumbling wheels vibrate its straining sides;
The huddled houses jostle up the hill,
They quote from many centuries and reigns,
Its narrow antique charm the street retains,
The growls of gridlocked cars its confines fill;
The new millennium - a chapter ends,
For volumes more our village book extends,
The warmth of memory, the treasured past,
The future's challenge, marvels unsurpassed;
A tightrope artist's skill, a balance true
Rewards and justifies our two way view.

John Tipton

The River Cam on the
approach to King's Mill

Mme. Alfred Carrière in full
flower on 'Old No.3'

Holy Trinity, the churchyard
and Mill Lane from the roof
of the Mill

ACKNOWLEDGEMENTS

The Parish Council, and the recorder in particular, offer sincere thanks to the following:
All those included for allowing the time to be photographed and write a few words, for giving encouragement and kind hospitality, lending or giving their own photographs and documents, for generously opening their doors, and not a few hearts...

John and Shirley Tipton for the excellent photographs of the Fête, the view of North End, the Littlebury Ladies meeting, also of Betty Starr, the Football, Cricket, and Bowls teams and clubs, and for writing about them, as well as about Cyril and Joyce Perrin, for their encouragement and interest and John in particular for his sonnet, light-heartedly requested, stunningly and unexpectedly delivered.

John Brownbridge of Saffron Walden for his beautiful work in binding and tooling this album and for his pictures of the electro fishing. Heikki Levhaslaiho for the digital photograph of the Brownies meeting. Nick Bouch and the Walden Local for supplying photographs of Mill Lane in flood and Tony Sweet and Trevor Fry for the use of the Littlebury Green Group photograph. The staff at 'Memories' in Saffron Walden for handling the processing of these photos with care and professionalism and Jenny Jones and the staff of the Office Services Department of Uttlesford District Council for kindly finding a window of opportunity for scanning both text and pictures.

Alan Granger for producing and supplying the superb map of the parish.

Jane Appleby for liasing with, and Alastair and Susan Lloyd for entertaining the members of the DCC at Granta House for an unscheduled ad hoc meeting so that their millennium album group photograph could be taken on an occasion that was a pleasure for all.

Robert and Sarah Bradfield, Elspeth Grant, Cynthia Lawrence, John and Laura MacGregor, Max and Gillian McGregor and Ruth Rigby for their generous donations towards the cost of the binding.

Sarah Aldrich, Judy Andrew, Jane Appleby, Andrew and Catherine Berisford, Jean Cowell, Michael and Harriet Christodoulides, Shirley Green, Valerie Green, Rose Johnson, Isabel Leeming, Alastair and Susan Lloyd, Pat Penney, Vicky Taylor, Graham Watson and Denis Wright for supplying information, checking and also writing pieces on the various committees of the parish.

On a personal note, to my fellow councillors for their enthusiasm and trust, sincere thanks. And finally, to my husband Sandy, not only for his photographs of the Parish Council, Village Hall Committee and the river, or for his own generous donation, but also to both he and our son Guy I offer heartfelt gratitude, for their constant support and encouragement, for generously accommodating my disappearances on many weekends and occasional weekdays this year, sometimes at short notice, for showing forbearance and patiently tolerating my word processing past several of Guy's bedtimes, a thousand thanks to you both.

Littlebury, December 2000

ACKNOWLEDGEMENTS ON PUBLICATION

That this book is published owes much to the energy and goodwill of many people. Even before the launch of the original document in February 2000, a call for it to be published was answered by the formation of a fundraising committee which came to be known as The Parish of Littlebury Millennium Society. This committee comprised Cynthia Lawrence, Pat Penney, Ruth Rigby, Bett Starr, June Sugden and Shirley Tipton, and was thankful for advice given on its constitution by Graham Watson.

Fund raising events included the launch itself, a Summer Brunch, a Christmas Party, a 'John Tipton' Quiz Night and close involvement with the Jubilee Celebrations held at The Queen's Head Inn. Additional help on these occasions was variously given by Jane Appleby, Jean Cowell, Celia Elmer, Claire Green and the Brownies, who also contributed generous prizes, Peggy Griggs, Minna Levhaslaiho, Susan Lloyd, Paul Marsh, Phyll McGrath, Barbara Mensforth, Cyril Perrin, Bryan Sugden, John Tipton, Sue Winterbottom and many volunteers and raffle prize givers along the way. Grateful thanks are offered to all these people and also, crucially, to those who attended the events, their encouragement underpinned the energy and resourcefulness of the members of the Society.

The Pink Ball Committee, a sub-committee of the society was formed. The members were: Sarah Aldrich, Carmel Carline, Julia Chapman, Ruth Farley, Rosie Juhl, Lucy Russell, Liz Stott, Jenny Walsh and Gillian Williamson. The Pink Ball was an ambitious project preceded by The Pink Bow Tie Coffee Morning hosted with elan by Gillian Williamson.

This Committee extends grateful thanks to its sponsors: Beaugrove, Blue, Camstead Homes, Country House Interiors, Dizzy Designs, ECMS, Gray Palmer, InterCounty, Keating Chambers, John and Laura MacGregor, National Westminster Bank, Quality Care, Ridgeons, R&R Saggers, Thermoteknix, The Tailor's Cat, Trevor Camp, Wendens Ambo Playgroup, and Wendens Ambo Mini Rugby Football Club.

Many kind favours were bestowed on The Pink Ball Committee, notably by Robert and Sarah Bradfield, Andrew Berisford, Jon and Jackie George and Jane Appleby. Bruce Munro, the givers of Promises, and the profligacy of our guests when bidding ensured an exciting and rewarding Auction of Promises. The dedication of the committee, some of whom live outside the parish, who cheerfully gave so much time creativity, and hard work was at the heart of this memorable summer's evening.

The Society owes a debt of gratitude for continued support from Uttlesford District Council's Ad Hoc Amenities Sub-Commitee and their two very welcome grants, Stuart Izzard of Community and Leisure for advice, Martin Housden and David Cammann at the Queen's Head Inn who also organised sponsorship which resulted in a substantial donation, for a most generous gift from the Saffron Walden Branch of The Round Table, the Stansted Airport Consultative Committee and Littlebury Parish Council for their donations, and Tesco.

Sincere appreciation is expressed for private donations received from the following: John Childs, Nicholas and Caroline Goulder, Elspeth Grant, Cynthia Lawrence, Bill and Isabel Leeming, Alastair and Susan Lloyd, Max and Gillian McGregor, Anthony and Janet Menell, Tim and Mary Seymour, Nigel and Pam Smith, Peter and Jenny Walsh, Laurie and Mollie Ward, and Graham and Janice Watson. Further, Francesca and Kinvara Hubbard, Harriet, James and Katie McCaffery, Guy Sanders and Emmanuele Kendrick all raised funds by sales of their toys. To have been in the capable hands of our talented designer Sally Powell with her painstaking eye for detail and those of Philip Dodd and his team at Healey's with their enthusiasm and skill has been our great good fortune.

Fundraising to print this book has been a true community effort, I have been inspired by the generosity of people and feel proud to have served with the Society and its Sub-Committee to this end and sincerely thank them, and again, my husband for his support which has been manifested in many ways. Since the Millennium year Littlebury Bridge has been strengthened, new houses have replaced the police houses and The Ranch House has been demolished to make way for three new homes. Littlebury Green playground has been refurbished and Catmere End finally has a sign. Already our record seems to be one of an age of innocence since we now grieve for those lost in the horror of September 11th. How lucky we are to be here. As our parish changes from the outside, within, it is hoped this sense of community will continue.

finis!